The Tyranny of Utility

The Tyranny of Utility

Behavioral Social Science and the Rise of Paternalism

Gilles Saint-Paul

PRINCETON UNIVERSITY PRESS

Princeton and Oxford

Published by Princeton University Press, 41 William Street, Princeton, New Jersey 08540
In the United Kingdom: Princeton University Press, 6 Oxford Street, Woodstock,
Oxfordshire OX20 1TW
press.princeton.edu

Library of Congress Cataloging-in-Publication Data

Saint-Paul, Gilles.
    The tyranny of utility : behavioral social science and the rise of paternalism / Gilles Saint-Paul.
        p.   cm.
    Includes bibliographical references and index.
    ISBN 978-0-691-12817-7 (hbk. : alk. paper) 1. Welfare economics. 2. Utilitarianism.
3. Paternalism. 4. Public welfare. I. Title.
    HB846.S25   2011
    330.12—dc22   2011003639

British Library Cataloging-in-Publication Data is available

This book has been composed in Minion Pro with Myriad Pro display

Printed on acid-free paper. ∞

Printed in the United States of America

10 9 8 7 6 5 4 3 2 1

Contents

Acknowledgments

This book has benefited from the careful reading of a number of anonymous reviewers, as well as from a lively conversation with Glen Weyl. I am grateful to them for encouraging me to try to make my book more accessible and for indicating useful references.

The Tyranny of Utility

Introduction

In the movie *Roman Holiday,* some of the most delightful scenes involve Gregory Peck and Audrey Hepburn riding an old scooter through the streets of Rome, and they seem to enjoy it thoroughly. We are all familiar with those images that have been reproduced and diffused to the point of becoming contemporary icons. Yet were the movie remade today, to remain realistic both protagonists would need to wear a helmet or else soon be arrested and fined by the police. As a result, the characters' scooter rides would be boring to them, and presumably even more so to the public.

What has changed is that there has been a (socially accepted) trend toward the increased regulation of private life. Armed with studies and statistics, government officials and their experts explain to us how greater coercion imposed on individual behavior saves that many lives or dollars. The press nods in approval. The underlying social science that supports those policies is rarely disputed, and the implicit social values that are being pursued are questioned even less. More than two hundred years ago, some enlightened intellectuals wrote the following in the French Declaration of Human Rights:

> Liberty consists in the freedom to do everything which injures no one else; hence the exercise of the natural rights of each man has no limits except those which assure to the other members of the society the enjoyment of the same rights.

This seems long forgotten. Instead of those enlightened intellectuals of the eighteenth century, we have experts who compute the optimal sugar content regulation of apple juice or the monetary equivalent of the welfare gains of wearing a helmet.

This essay discusses the rise of paternalistic policies and their dangers. It specifically relates this phenomenon to parallel developments in the social sciences. Although some believe that such intellectual debates are confined to academia's ivory tower and irrelevant to real-world policies, historical precedents suggest otherwise. The ethno-nationalist states of the late nineteenth century and the first half of the twentieth century, which culminated in Nazism, were prepared by a long academic tradition, especially in Germany, which emphasized

Volkisch values at the expense of universal ones. Immediately after World War II, most of Eastern Europe fell to communism, and many Western European countries were about to follow that route. At that time Hayek pointed out how these developments had been prepared by socialist biases in universities. And, finally, the belief in free markets of many "liberal" decision makers rests only on the positivist view taught by mainstream economists—that "science" has proved "it works."

Similarly, the recent development of paternalism is not devoid of intellectual apparatus. Of all the social sciences, economics is the one that has traditionally stuck to the individualistic values of the Enlightenment. But in recent years a new brand of economics (labeled "behavioral") departs from those foundations and brings new ammunition to state involvement in private lives. The aim of this book is to explain what behavioral economics is and whether it is dangerous for those who believe in individual freedom and limited government.

It is generally accepted that intellectuals, including scientists, are supposed to be "concerned citizens" in addition to pursuing truth and contributing to knowledge. The economist is no exception, and many prospective graduate students, in their motivation letters, routinely claim, for example, that they want to "make the world a better place." On the other hand, a popular view of economists is that they typically support "free markets," "free trade," and limited government. How can one hold such views and at the same time pretend to improve the situation of one's fellow citizens?

The answer lies in the long tradition of so-called neoclassical economics, which is grounded on utilitarianism. Utilitarianism states that "society" should be organized so as to yield the greatest possible level of welfare, where it is assumed that there is some way of comparing and adding welfare across individuals. Adam Smith's famous invisible hand states that a maximum level of total welfare is reached by letting people decide what is best for them. In the nineteenth century, followers of Smith such as Ricardo, Pareto, and Walras established "scientific" results that led credence to the invisible hand view. By "scientific" I mean that it was possible to prove, in a mathematical way, that under some assumptions—made explicit by the use of the scientific method— free markets indeed lead to an efficient outcome where welfare, in some sense, is at a maximum.

These assumptions are mathematical statements about how human behavior is being analyzed by economic theory. But they are also, inevitably, moral statements about what the individual is. For the invisible hand to make sense (i.e., for those results to hold), individuals should be unitary (have consistent goals and preferences) and rational (make the right decisions, given their constraints and information, in order to satisfy their preferences). In other words, they know where their interest lies and are capable of pursuing it.

Therefore, neoclassical economics draws a bridge between the positivist perspective of a would-be benevolent dictator attempting to design society optimally, and the liberal perspective of a political philosopher of the Enlightenment, for whom preserving individual rights and keeping government in check is a crucial goal.

This alliance has held firm for more than a century, whereas other intellectual disciplines have witnessed pervasive attacks against the view that individuals are unitary and rational. As a result, neoclassical economics has found itself increasingly isolated, both methodologically and as a promoter of liberal eighteenth-century values such as limited government.

More recently economics itself is gradually discarding the unitary individual, while keeping its utilitarian perspective on government. As a result, it is providing ammunition to an ongoing process of growing government intrusion in private lives, a key component of which consists of paternalistic policies aimed at protecting people against themselves. This joint development is what this book is about.

The mathematical results about the merits of laissez-faire are an attempt to *scientifically* validate limited governments on pure utilitarian considerations. We are not told that excess government involvement in private matters is wrong; we are simply told that it *does not work*. That, in a way, is laudable, to the extent that we do not want an analytical discipline to be polluted by ethical or ideological a priori.

Unfortunately science, unlike moral principles, evolves quickly; a theory is unlikely to survive for long if its predictions (or premises) are inconsistent with the empirical evidence. Virtually none of the theories that prevailed in the nineteenth century, whether in the natural or social sciences, is accepted today. And therefore it was only natural that sooner or later the economics on which the "scientific" foundation for individual freedom rests would be challenged on empirical grounds.

These empirical developments undermine the view that individuals are rational, consistent and capable of self-control. They bring economics in line with other intellectual traditions (which had challenged the unitary nature of the individual long before economics); at the same time they invalidate the "theorems" that tell us that laissez-faire works well. Since, under the dominant positivist assumptions, this was the main reason why we believed in laissez-faire, this opens the door for the pervasive intrusion of government in private affairs.

In his *Road to Serfdom,* Hayek (1944) links the suppression of individual freedom to the well-meaning attempt by intellectuals to "make the world a better place." The issue, then, was how the government could better allocate material resources by coordinating the economic decisions of individual agents. This, Hayek argued, could only come at the cost of a dictatorship. Fortunately, somehow, the dictatorships that engaged in central planning, despite their suppression of virtually all liberties, miserably failed as economic coordinators— even by their own purely materialistic and quantitative standards. The theoretical idea that governments could improve the lives of people through central planning had been refuted by a tough reality test: the partisans of dirigisme would be quiet for a while, unless they found another theory.

Another theory? This is exactly what the above-mentioned developments, with their attack on the consistent, rational view of the individual, give them, and they lost no time in making use of it. While a new brand of economics—so-called behavioral economics—provides foundations for much broader government interventions than before, at the same time we see increased government attempts at regulating individual behavior in matters such as consumption, saving, education, risk taking, and speech. Just as traditional economics could be viewed as an important intellectual cornerstone of the Enlightenment's "liberal" society, behavioral economics will contribute to the foundation of the new paternalistic state.

As this book will make clear, my opinion is that this is cause for serious concern. If current trends continue, I foresee a gradual elimination of individual freedom as "social science" makes progress in documenting behavioral biases, measuring happiness, and evaluating the effects of coercive policies, while information technology provides ever more efficient tools of control to the government.

A central conclusion of this book is that these developments are the inevitable consequence of the utilitarian agenda of defining the limits of government in a purely scientific fashion, based on the search for an efficient allocation of resources from the point of view of a social welfare function which aggregates individual preferences. Furthermore, because the empirical evidence for behavioral biases is pervasive, one cannot restore the traditional brand of utilitarianism as a foundation for limited governments. Nor can one preserve individual freedom by dismissing paternalistic policies on purely practical grounds by arguing that their implementation is counterproductive. Instead, individual freedom and responsibility must be recognized as central social values rather than as derived as instruments for implementing the calculus of happiness.

Part I

The Demise of the Unitary Individual

1

Political Organization and the Conception of Man

The state is man writ large. —Plato

Westerners are proud of their political institutions. They associate them with a high material standard of living, a great variety of individual choices, freedom of speech, and checks and balances that prevent governments from drifting toward despotism. Because these institutions are so satisfying, they are tempted to believe that they are universal. That means that they are not inherent to the West and could be adopted by any culture, without that culture being changed. It is such a view, for example, that underlines the (now somewhat discredited) neoconservative agenda of spreading democracy to the Middle East. Some people disagree with this agenda because they think that democracy and the related institutions in which we believe are actually part of our culture, and that another culture could not adopt it without first changing itself. Both Japan and Turkey, for example, underwent a long phase of Westernization before becoming actual (and far from perfect) democracies.

A culture influences the determination of political institutions through many channels. One is its conception of Man. The "liberal"[1] political institutions that we seem to cherish are inherited from the Enlightenment and its conception of Man, which is itself the outcome of a long evolution in the history of thought, from Aristotle to Christianity, to the Renaissance and the Reformation. This tradition states that the individual is autonomous and his aspirations respectable. That is why it places much emphasis on individual rights and has given birth to Lockean theories of governments where the legitimacy of power is grounded in the consent of individuals to participate in a social contract rather than some immanent divine order.

This conception is so pervasive in our society that we are not even aware of it, for a number of reasons. Our daily practice of democracy tends to trivialize it. We risk turning it into a consumer good, ignoring its cultural and philosophical foundations. Above all, our relative contempt for intellectuals leads

---

[1] Throughout the book I shall use the word "liberal" with the traditional English/French meaning, and not with the more recent American meaning which refers to holding left-wing views.

us to forget that these institutions were designed by them, and reflect their conceptions.

Although we take our individualist philosophy for granted, even in the West it was not prevalent in a not-so-distant past. In ancient times the individual's well-being was entirely subordinate to that of the tribe. Individuals were just functional elements of a wider collective machine, and all that mattered was the tribe's power and capacity to survive. The scope for individual choice was trivial compared to the resources, efforts, and sacrifices that were imposed on the people in the name of the community. In the Republic of Sparta a man had the right to live only if he could prove to be sufficiently strong, and he then had to devote his life to the army. For the Spartans, the individual is just a vector for the genes of the tribe. The social organization is designed so as to make the best use of these vectors for the purpose of obtaining as much power as possible for the tribe. Individual goals and aspirations are largely irrelevant.

The individual emancipated himself from the tribe with the advent of Christianity, which presents itself as a personal religion rather than the religion of a tribe, a state, or a nation, and furthermore introduces the notion of free will. This set the stage for the liberal political philosophies of the seventeenth and eighteenth centuries, which are explicitly based upon the individual. It is instructive to note, in this context, how the political systems proposed by these philosophies are matched with a theory of the individual. To take the most prominent cases, both Locke and Hobbes consider the individual as conscious, self-aware, and rational, and base their political philosophies on these views. However, these two individualists differ about the nature of Man, and so do their favorite political systems. Man, according to Hobbes, is a predator, and civil peace can only be reached if he surrenders all his natural rights to the state. For that reason Hobbes advocates an absolute monarchy. For Locke, man is intrinsically good, and the political system should be designed to allow people to fulfill their individual aspirations. He therefore advocates that government's main role should be to arbitrate contractual disputes between individuals, and that governments should be organized along the principles of representative democracy and the separation of powers.

Freedom and Responsibility

A cornerstone of liberal thought is that individual freedom is inseparable from individual responsibility. Voltaire said: "My freedom stops where that of others starts." This powerful statement tells us that in order to be operative, freedom must have well-defined boundaries. This goes so far that the American Constitution and the 1789 French Declaration of Human Rights do not define freedom so much by what you may do (positive rights) but rather by what may *not* be done to you (negative rights);—freedom, in other words, is defined by its boundaries, not by its contents. Equally important are the boundaries set on the government's freedom. Thus the Habeas Corpus act of 1679 restricts the power of the state by preventing people from being imprisoned without due trial.

Mill (1863) proposes a concise definition of the limits to both individual and government actions, which arguably would lead to the maximum possible degree of freedom:

> The sole end for which mankind are warranted, individually or collectively, in interfering with the liberty of action of any of their number, is self-protection. [...] the only purpose for which power can be rightfully exercised over any member of a civilized community, against his will, is to prevent harm to others. [...] The only part of the conduct of any one, for which he is amenable to society, is that which concerns others. [...] Over himself, over his own body and mind, the individual is sovereign.

Although problems start when one tries to define more precisely what is meant by "harm," "self-protection," and even "others," this definition epitomizes the liberal approach to civil liberties.

The negative rights approach to freedom has many virtues. First, it means that one may do anything provided the boundaries are respected. If a constitution specifies my right to do so and so, how shall I interpret it if I want to do otherwise? Second, it prevents any ambiguity, and therefore any conflict, in exercising a right. It is always feasible for me not to trespass my neighbor's premises, and vice versa.

In contrast, in modern-day social democracies, there is a sense that freedom is defined by "positive rights," meaning that people are entitled to a certain *outcome*, regardless of whether they can afford it or whether they have taken any steps in the past to achieve it on their own. Thus one now talks about the right to education, the right to housing, the right to a bank account, the right to an Internet connection, and so on. Such positive rights will typically lead to conflict. They are, in fact, obligations imposed on others that violate their own rights. At a minimum they compel the state to levy more taxes in order to finance these "rights" for those who claim it. Although such taxes dilute the costs of enforcing positive rights, they do not abolish the conflicts and contradictions inherent to them. If all citizens were to stop working and claim their right to housing, nobody would be left to build these houses, and there would be no tax base to finance them. Moreover, the increment in taxes needed to fund the positive rights of some claimants may violate the positive rights of others. What if I can no longer afford my apartment because of the additional taxes? Isn't that a violation of my own right to housing?

Positive rights are enforceable only if others agree or are forced to bear their material consequences. Positive rights are an infringement on Voltaire's principle and do not constitute freedom. It is telling that the only positive right granted in the American Declaration of Independence is the "pursuit of happiness," which has no well-defined material counterpart and does not imply obligations for others.

Thus freedom, as defined by the Enlightenment, has the merit of being operational. But it is not enough to have an operational definition. We also need that definition—that is, the boundaries of freedom—to be enforced. There comes the notion of responsibility. Individuals must be liable for their infringements of other people's rights. Otherwise there will be no punishment for violating them and no freedom in practice. It is because individuals are considered to be responsible that the legal system can work as an incentive to respect other people's rights.

That freedom is inseparable from responsibility can be seen by considering one without the other. Responsibility without freedom is oppression. It is the world depicted by ancient Greek tragedies and by the novels of Franz Kafka. In Greek tragedies, people are bound by laws and codes of honor that they have not made and that entirely specify their behavior. The tragedy arises because these social norms contradict each other (as in *Antigone* by Sophocles) or because their enforcement has absurd and lethal consequences (as in the *Atrides* by Aeschylus); in the extreme case, one may be held guilty for actions of which one is not even aware. Oedipus is condemned for having copulated with his mother and murdered his father, unknowingly. And Joseph K. is guilty of a crime that will never be revealed to him, and not even to the reader. In more modern days, innocent girls in tribal zones of Pakistan or Nigeria are being lapidated for adultery, despite the adultery having been committed against their will because they were raped. Responsibility without freedom is characteristic of the societies for whom the individual is not an autonomous being but just a member of a tribe. Rules are made for the welfare of the tribe, independently of any concept of interpersonal justice or individual welfare.

Freedom without responsibility is extortion. It is the world of modern welfare states where people claim compensation for situations in which they willingly put themselves—single parenthood, undersaving, inappropriate educational choices, quitting one's job, and so on. That does not mean, of course, that all people who get benefits from the welfare state put themselves in a bad situation purposely. But we do observe that welfare states discriminate very little along those lines when distributing benefits, and we want to understand why. When freedom without responsibility is not mediated by the welfare state, its contradictions become more obvious, as the costs are more apparent and are imposed on a subset of us rather than diluted through the tax system. One illustration is the squat movement, by which a group of people seizes someone else's property and lives there, on the ground that "they need it" and that it is "empty." In many countries of continental Europe, it turns out to be very difficult to expel the squatters because of a positive "right to housing."[2] As a result, the owner cannot

---

[2] See, for example, http://www.ehow.com/facts_7342546_squatters_-rights-spain.html for a brief discussion of the protection of squatters in Spain from 1980 to 1996; one could also check the Wikipedia entry on the squat movement (http://en.wikipedia.org/wiki/Squatting) which in my view is largely sympathetic to squatting and rests on the implicit assumption that housing is a positive right.

use it for himself or rent it to a tenant—the squatter's "right to housing" is violating somebody else's "right to housing." In a similar vein, a "humanitarian" association had distributed tents to homeless people in France and established camps (near shantytowns) in highly visible spots in central parts of the country's major cities. Not only do these people disregard common rules and appropriate the public space but they bypass local agreements by which nomadic people should stay in designated areas, generally at the periphery of the city. So what if Gypsies, who generally abide by these agreements, now claim that they, too, want to stay in a public garden at the center of the city? Given the relative scarcity of such space, it is not possible to satisfy all these conflicting claims, even ignoring the violation of everybody's basic right to circulate in public areas. In many instances, the homeless were offered the chance to relocate in more attractive shelters in peripheral districts but refused to do so. At stake here is not the right to fulfill one's basic needs but the right to do as one pleases while not being liable for the harmful consequences imposed on others.[3]

This discussion illustrates how any workable system of civil liberties must rest on individual responsibility. But individual responsibility only works if people are rational and have free will. Free will means that they can choose any of the feasible alternatives they face. Alternatively, they could be driven by instinct, act randomly because they are insane, or be determined, as were the heroes of Greek tragedies, by powerful social norms that eliminate any scope for choice. Rationality means that people can compute the consequences of their actions, are sufficiently informed to do so, and act in their own best interest. For example, if people do not realize that going to jail harms them, then they have no reason to abstain from committing a crime.

Therefore the liberal system which we have inherited from the Enlightenment only makes sense if one adheres to the conception of Man as a rational individual endowed with free will.[4] The more we go away from this conception, the more difficult it is to abide by a constitution based on individual responsibility,

---

[3] A different issue is the extent to which one should redistribute to the needy. This is further discussed in chapter 3, but clearly there is no a priori contradiction between such redistribution and enforcing individual responsibility. My observation here is that, over time, we observe a deconditioning of welfare payments on individual choices, and therefore a lower enforcement of individual responsibility; this, however, is a matter of public debate at least in the area of unemployment benefits, where conditionality is often advocated and sometimes implemented.

[4] Indeed, Mill claims that his defense of individual freedom only applied to sufficiently advanced societies where individuals can be expected to behave in such a reasonable fashion: "For the same reason, we may leave out of consideration those backward states of society in which the race itself may be considered as in its nonage. The early difficulties in the way of spontaneous progress are so great, that there is seldom any choice of means for overcoming them; and a ruler full of the spirit of improvement is warranted in the use of any expedients that will attain an end, perhaps otherwise unattainable. Despotism is a legitimate mode of government in dealing with barbarians, provided the end be their improvement." Thus, in just two sentences, Mill is destroying his entire argument in favor of freedom and against paternalism. For who is going to judge the extent to which people are "backward," if not the rulers and their associated "experts"?

the more blurred the frontier between one's rights and other people's rights, and the lower the degree of freedom that can be reached.

For individuals to be rational it must be that they are *unitary*—in other words, they have a unique "self." That means that their behavior is driven by consistent preferences which allows them to rank alternatives. Otherwise, the very notion of their best interest would not be defined. By consistent, we mean that the preferences should satisfy two requirements. First, the same individual always chooses according to the same set of preferences. This should not be confused with saying that the same individual will make the same choices on Mondays and on Tuesdays. One can have a consistent preference for pizza on Monday and ice cream on Tuesday. Inconsistency arises, say, if on Monday the individual decides to have an ice cream on Tuesday but will change his mind the day after (despite no new information arriving) and go for a pastry instead. Second, preferences must lead to a well-defined set of most preferred actions in all the situations in which the individual may encounter himself. This criterion imposes restrictions, discussed later in the book when we analyze how economics has emerged as a bastion of rationality within the social sciences.

For now, it is enough to note that not all preferences are consistent. An individual who prefers A to B, B to C, and C to A is capable of choosing between any pair of these three choices but incapable of choosing if offered the three possibilities simultaneously.[5] His preferences are not consistent and he cannot be rational. The same can be said of an individual who, like Dr. Jekyll and Mr. Hyde, has several conflicting incarnations. The choices made by Mr. Hyde during the night harm Dr. Jekyll during the day. This composite individual is not unitary: there is no meaningful sense in which one could say that he acts in his own interest. If people are not unitary but instead, like Stevenson's monster, consist of several incarnations, imposing the discipline of individual responsibility on them fails both morally and operationally. It is unfair to punish Dr. Jekyll for the deeds of Mr. Hyde, and it does not work to threaten Dr Jekyll with punishment to convince Mr. Hyde to act otherwise.

▍Two Challenges to the Unitary Individual

The main attacks on liberal values since the eighteenth century have come from collectivist ideologies and political systems that resemble the value systems of ancient times in that they endorse the supremacy of the tribe over the individual. The nationalistic ideologies of the nineteenth century and their twentieth-century offspring, Fascism and Nazism, come immediately to mind. For the Nazis the relevant ethical and political unit is the race, not the individual. Not only did the Nazis pursue the subjugation of competing races, but they also

---

[5] This is why economists impose the restriction on preferences that they must be transitive, that is, that such a configuration must not arise.

practiced the elimination of unfit individuals within their own race, in the fashion of the Spartans. When Hitler learned of the fall of Stalingrad, he could not understand why the top commanders had not committed suicide: "What is Life? Life is the Nation. The individual must die anyway."[6]

Similarly, for the Communists, the basic unit is social class, not the individual. Once these two ideologies restored a collectivist system of values for their political system, they could easily deprive individuals of their freedom, property, and life. Moreover, collectivist ideologies could now appeal to science. Nazism can be founded on Darwinian considerations, especially when Darwinism claims that the basic unit of selection is the gene rather than the individual organism. Communism rests on historical and economic determinism.

Although grounded in a very different tradition, the principles of the French Revolution are not that remote from such tribalism. Its notion of self-government is based on Rousseau's fiction of a general will, which rules out any consideration for disagreement between individuals and leads at best to the dictature of the majority.

Somewhat paradoxically, we have also experienced another, parallel evolution that goes in exactly the opposite direction. The legitimacy of the individual was increasingly challenged not only on the grounds that the individual is "too small" but also on the grounds that it is "too large." The individual, in other words, is made of psychological sub-units that may contradict one another and therefore need not aggregate into a coherent self. Under the impulse of Romanticism, Western thought gradually moved away from the Cartesian ego to replace it by conflicting processes that undermine the notions of free will and rational preferences. This evolution can be seen in various contexts, as in the philosophies of Nietzsche, Freud, or the postmodernists, or the literary works of Proust, Joyce, or the surrealists.

One should be cautious about dismissing these trends as having no practical influence. Constitutions are written by intellectuals. This intellectual evolution, if translated into a political doctrine, jeopardizes the whole Lockean system of political organization, because that system rests on the existence and legitimacy of rational individual aspirations, and on the applicability of individual responsibility.

[6] Cited by Beevor 1998.

2

The Challenge to the Unitary Individual
in Western Thought

In the nineteenth century various strands of thought started challenging the hypothesis of a rational unitary individual and eventually achieved considerable influence. One prominent critic was Nietzsche. For Nietszche, the individual's attempt to develop a consistent self and to make sense of and conceptualize objective reality is a miserable lie that is socially constructed by weaker individuals in order to rationalize their lack of vitality. One can be connected with reality, if it exists, only through instinct, intuition, and the senses, and that experience can transcend its pure animal nature only to the extent that it can be turned into an aesthetic one. Concepts and reason, alternatively, are just a collection of metaphors that remain hopelessly confined within that abstraction, the language, which as such is not capable of providing a basis for a worthwhile life.[1]

A concise statement of such views can be found in *The Will to Power* (1889), in which he views the individual as consisting of multiple, conflicting selves:

> The assumption of one single subject is perhaps unnecessary; perhaps it is just as permissible to assume a multiplicity of subjects, whose interaction and struggle is the basis of our thought and our consciousness in general? A kind of aristocracy of "cells" in which dominion resides? To be sure, an aristocracy of equals, used to ruling jointly and understanding how to command?
> My hypotheses: The subject as multiplicity.

This vision of the self, along with claims about the inability of reason and concepts to truly grasp reality, leads Nietzsche to condemn the liberal society of the Enlightenment, which rests on the illusory world of concepts in which true human fulfillment cannot be attained. Since freedom, constitutions, and human rights are concepts, it is not surprising that the alternative system proposed by Nietzsche is in radical contradiction to that of Locke, Voltaire, and Mill. Since

---

[1] See *On Truth and Lies in a Nonmoral Sense* (1873).

there is no longer a foundation for reciprocity and respect for others' property and physical integrity, it is acceptable for individuals with superior vitality to infringe on the rights of lesser beings (and calling this an infringement is itself but a delusive abstraction).

Accordingly, the human ideal proposed by Nietzsche rejects self-consciousness which is another illusory property of the language; therefore there is no sense in which he would be unitary or even care about optimizing his behavior according to consistent preferences. He is some kind of beast (the "blonde beast") who gives in to his instincts and the immediate stimuli of his environment.

It is interesting to compare Nietzsche's point of view with that of the ancient Greek philosophers. They, too, were aware of the behavioral limitations of the real-world individuals. Aristotle defined as *akrasia* a range of behaviors driven by instinct and in contradiction with reason or self-interest. This can take the form of either weakness or impetuosity, and be driven by either anger or pleasure. However, the Greeks considered *akrasia* both as a defect that could and should be overcome and as an analytical difficulty in their conception of man as a unitary being.[2] In contrast, Nietzsche's deconstruction of the rational self is a centerpiece of his whole system.

Nietzsche's thought had numerous influences, most notably on Freudianism and the late twentieth century's Postmodernists.

▌ Freud

Sigmund Freud's psychoanalysis is a "science" of the mind which is explicitly based on the self being multiple. The theory is well known since it has been popularized by numerous books and movies. People are made of two selves: a conscious and an unconscious one. The conscious self is the by-product of education and is considered by Freud as rational and consistent. But the unconscious self "wants" something else—according to Freud, this something else is made of primitive pulsions (incest and murder) that civilization has had to repress in order to survive. In the world of psychoanalysis, people face a difficult choice. Either (as Mr. Hyde) I give in to my unconscious pulsions and I become a sociopath, or I repress them and I become a psychopath. In other words, individual fulfillment becomes impossible, because pursuing rational, conscious goals comes at the cost of repressing the irrational, unconscious pulsions and generates neuroses.

Although Freud himself was a social conservative and did not advocate inconsistent or harmful behavior, his theory has been much used to condone such behavior in various contexts. Arguably the increased popularity of psychoanalysis in the second half of the twentieth century has given rise to a host of characters indulging in erratic behavior on the grounds that they need to cope with

---

[2] I am indebted to an anonymous reviewer for drawing my attention to Aristotle's position.

their neuroses.[3] This exemplifies how a theory—which, incidentally, is constructed so as not to be scientifically provable—eventually permeates popular representations and ultimately affects human behavior.

▎ Science

The challenges to the rational, unitary conception of the individual that come from philosophical systems could easily be dismissed as reflecting the mood of their time. Far more serious are the criticisms that science, and neuroscience in particular, can throw at the unitary individual, since one is now talking about experimental evidence that people do not behave in a consistent way.[4]

Neuroscientists view the brain as a space where several processes compete so as to effect the organism's behavior. Processes can be either controlled or automatic, and they can be either cognitive or affective. The distinction between controlled and automatic is very much like the distinction between conscious and unconscious. Controlled processes intervene when one decides which car to buy, which moves to play next in a chess game, and in which pension fund one should put one's savings. Automatic processes include object recognition, dreams, and the trajectory of your hand when you are reaching an object.

The existence of automatic processes is already a problem for the unitary view: when driven by such processes, individuals may perform an action despite having made a rational decision against it; such an action may run against their objective interest—it might lead them to jail, for example, and it may contradict previous choices that the individual may have made.

The distinction between cognitive processes and affective processes is another source of inconsistent behavior. There is a hotel in London where the customer will find a complimentary jug full of candies in his room. When I go there I typically eat half the candies; if I had been asked whether I would like the candies to be in my room at the time I made my reservation, I would have said no. The affective process which makes me like sweet food is in conflict with the cognitive process which tells me I will take weight on. Neuroscience says that one process has to overrule the other and that this depends on the circumstances. One day I may have the nerve to throw the candy jug into the trash can; the next day I would indulge and eat the candies. How, then, can one measure the degree of my taste for them? It is not even a well-defined concept.

Cognitive and affective systems may collaborate or conflict depending on the intensity of affect. At a low intensity collaboration prevails, in that affective

[3] As a typical example, most characters in Woody Allen's comedies are incapable of committing to a stable romantic relationship, because such commitment is superseded by soul-searching and the elusive search for self-realization (which may be interpreted, however, as an excuse for remaining on the dating market in the hope of finding a more attractive mate).

[4] The discussion that follows draws extensively on a paper by Camerer, Loewenstein, and Prelec 2005.

systems provide useful information to cognitive ones in order to make decisions. For example, if I feel unsafe in my neighborhood I will make the rational decision to move to another place. At intermediate intensities, the conflicts described in the above example about the candy jug arise. At a high level of intensity, emotions overrule the cognitive system in a harmful way, leading to phenomena such as fainting, bursts of violence, and the like.

Worse, then, the uncontrolled affective system is itself made of conflicting processes. In the above example, a controlled cognitive system (planning for one's calorie intake) fights with an uncontrolled system driven by physical pleasure. But Berridge (1996) has found evidence of _raw motivation_ for performing certain actions; that is, these actions are executed despite the fact that they might bring no pleasure, and even might bring pain, while also not being part of a rational decision plan. In other words, these actions fulfill neither short-run nor long-term needs. In the words of Camerer and colleagues, "Berridge believes that the later stages of many drug addictions present prototypical examples of situations of what he terms 'wanting' without 'liking'; drug addicts often report a complete absence of pleasure from taking the drug they are addicted to, coupled with an irresistible motivation to do so." They then outline a potential policy conclusion which may lay ground for the paternalistic interventions discussed later in the book. "If wanting and liking are two separate processes, then it cannot be assumed that satisfying someone's desires necessarily makes them better off."

It also has been found that processes of different types activate different areas in the brain; automatic processes tend to take place in the back and controlled processes lie in the front. Thus the brain itself is not unitary in a spatial sense; rather, it resembles a military map where conflicting armies occupy different areas in order to get their best chances in the battle.

The challenge to the unitary view of the individual is clear: automatic processes evolved millions of years ago to help us deal with situations that are quite different from those we encounter in the contemporary world. Because they are uncontrolled they drive a number of our actions that an optimizing, controlled cognitive process would not have decided. That conflict would not have existed in the hunter-gatherer societies that prevailed when the automatic processes evolved, for controlled processes then presumably "shared the same goals" as automatic processes. Inconsistency in behavior thus reflects the differences between the environment faced by our ancestors and ours.

While automatic processes may be the source of conflicting motivations and goals, and thus lead to inconsistent or self-harming behavior, they also affect our capacity to learn and make correct inferences on the basis of the signals we receive from our environment. Neuroscientists have shown that the learning process is associated with permanent physiological modifications of our brain. As a consequence, phenomena arise that tend to prevent rational learning. It has been found that people tend to believe messages that are repeated even though they know that the message is false. According to Ross, Leppner, and

Hubbard (1995), "when people form beliefs based on evidence that is later discredited definitively, the belief founded on the discredited evidence persists." Another aspect is the mind's propensity to rationalize and make sense of actions that are actually driven by automatic processes. Evidence suggests that the brain activity associated with an action starts *before* one is actually aware of having the intention to perform the action. And there are experiences where one electrically stimulates a brain zone associated with laughter, and the patient systematically finds explanations for her behavior.

Recent developments in neurosciences, rather than supporting the unitary view of the individual, depict a world where *akrasia* is pervasive and are even somewhat supportive of Nietzsche's nihilistic positions. They suggest that people act as if they were pursuing contradictory goals, that they are incapable of making rational use of their information, and that even the simple notion of intent may be considered spurious.

3

Economics: The Last Bastion of Rationality

Many people traditionally think of economists as advocates of laissez-faire, that is, letting the free operation of markets determine how resources are allocated throughout society. Where does this presumption come from? It comes from some central results of economic theory which predict that, in some sense, free markets lead to desirable outcomes from the point of view of global efficiency.

Essentially these results come from two observations. First, competitive markets allow all voluntary transactions to take place. Second, all voluntary transactions are mutually advantageous and therefore increase the welfare of both parties. A competitive equilibrium is a situation where, given prices, people undertake all the transactions that they deem profitable, and such that, furthermore, these transactions are globally feasible—meaning that markets clear. At a competitive equilibrium, the scope for improvements has been exhausted: any transaction that is mutually advantageous is either already taking place or is not feasible; that is why total welfare is at a maximum. Essential to this conclusion is the assumption that individuals are unitary.

In this chapter I discuss how the assumptions underlying economic theory lead to a presumption of laissez-faire, and why this apparatus is fragile because those assumptions are not grounded on empirical observations but on methodological requirements instead. I revisit the central concepts and results of traditional, utilitarian welfare economics in light of their implications for limited government, and individual freedom and responsibility.

Homo economicus

The central concept used by economists in describing human behavior is that of *utility*. Utility is the number of units of "welfare," or "happiness," that an individual gets as a result of his situation. The greater number of units I get, the "happier" I am. Thus if a fishing trip delivers 5 units and a ski holiday delivers 10, I prefer the ski holiday over the fishing trip.

A crucial assumption is that my utility only depends on my own objective situation. Thus I can get more or less units of welfare depending on where I live, what I consume, what I do for a living, and so forth; but what my neighbours do, the poverty rate in a remote country, or the contents of a book I will not read are all irrelevant to me unless they affect my own situation through some mechanism. The *utility function* is a mathematical object that tells us how many units of happiness each possible situation yields for the individual.

People must make decisions, and they face constraints. These constraints include physical laws (I cannot decide to become weightless or to fly faster than the speed of light) and institutional restrictions such as the legal environment or the binding contracts they have signed. People also have a budget constraint which essentially implies that they cannot consume more than they produce. These constraints define what the individual can and cannot do. Economics assume that an individual is a *Homo economicus.* This means that he evaluates all his feasible choices and picks the one associated with the highest level of utility. Because *Homo economicus* has a utility function, he can actually use it to compute how many units of happiness are associated with each option. Thus the assumption that people have a utility function implies that they can consistently choose between alternatives, and their decisions are entirely determined by their utility function and the constraints they face.

unitary The individual is unitary in the sense that his utility function is unique. This means that no matter how many decisions the individual has to make, he will try to maximize the same utility function each time he has to make one of those decisions. People have a unique utility function just as they have a unique liver, nose, or stomach. Their behavior, in particular, is not driven by competing brain processes or "selves" that would alternatively get the upper hand. That an individual's behavior is driven by his utility function implies that his behavior is consistent in several ways. One important aspect is that he has no incentive to renege on it. That does not mean that he will always act the same. I may well have had a veal cutlet yesterday for lunch and yet prefer a pizza today. But if asked, I will not regret my choice of a veal cutlet yesterday. It may turn out not to be terribly good, so that, had I known better, I would have had a pizza instead. But I did not have that information when making my choice; lack of regret means that, if put back in time and facing the same circumstances and the same information, I will again order a veal cutlet. From my unique utility function one may predict my choices at all times and in all circumstances.

Two important properties can illustrate the kind of consistency requirements that economic theory imposes on preferences. First, preferences are *transitive.* This simply means that if I prefer to go to the opera rather than buying a new pair of shoes, and if I prefer a new TV set over going to the opera, then I favor the TV set over the pair of shoes. This means that I not only can perform pairwise comparisons but that I am also capable of making a choice for any set of alternatives presented to me. An individual without transitive preferences would be somehow "crazy" and could not make consistent choices. If I prefer the TV set over the opera, the opera over the pair of shoes, and the pair of shoes over the TV set, there is no way I can make a decision if faced with the three alternatives. One can show that such situations cannot occur if people have a unique utility function.

Second, preferences should be *independent of the context*. In particular, my preference between the TV set and the opera does not depend on the order in which I consider them, nor does it depend on the other choices available to me: I prefer the TV set over the opera regardless of whether a pair of shoes is available. This property is called "independence of irrelevant alternatives." In particular, the way information is being presented has no effect on individual choices, and individuals are always better off with more alternatives than with fewer—the only way new alternatives can affect their behavior is if they discard their previous choices in favor of the newly available ones. This means, however, that the new decision yields more utility than the previous one, so that the individual's welfare necessarily increases. Similarly, more information is always better than less information: I can always ignore the new information and reach the same decision and welfare level as if it had not been available; if using the new information changes my behavior, it must be because it makes me better off.

In its purest form, economics does not assert how people actually behave. It has nothing to say about whether people prefer live theater to a movie, apples to oranges, or consuming today versus later. The only restrictions it places on human behavior are that it be consistent and that it be compatible with the existence of economic equilibrium (that is, there exists a set of prices such that supply equals demand in all markets). Thus the psychological traits that are assumed are the ones that are minimal for the theory to work; the economist's vision of individual behavior is derived from methodological requirements rather than empirical observation.

To understand the interplay between the methodological construct of a theory and the assumptions made about human psychology, it is useful to consider a typical requirement which is imposed on the utility function: that of *concavity*. Typically it means that as more of a good is consumed, additional units yield lower incremental utility. Economists typically assume that is true not because they believe it is an iron law of human behavior, but because it allows them to prove some important results, namely, that a competitive equilibrium where all markets clear simultaneously exists. If utility fails to be concave, one is not certain that an equilibrium exists, and a cornerstone of the theory disappears.

The assumption of concavity is intuitively plausible: we indeed expect people to be fed up if they get too much of the same. But it is not made because it is plausible, or because it is a general trait of human psychology—indeed, it is perfectly conceivable that one prefers to increase one's consumption of at least some goods at high levels than at low levels, at least over some range. It is made because it delivers the result that an equilibrium where markets clear exists. It is a stronger restriction than transitivity: as seen above, a unitary individual necessarily has transitive preferences; however, a unitary individual may not have a concave utility.

The kind of restrictions described here are fit for simple models where one has to make a choice between consuming, say, apples versus tomatoes. These restrictions typically have to be extended when one wants to apply the economics framework to more complex issues where intertemporal choice and risk are involved. Let us describe how intertemporal choice is handled, since it is one of the main aspects of economic theory that is challenged by behavioral approaches.

For intertemporal choice to be consistent it must again derive from a unique, timeless utility function. This guarantees that my decisions do not depend on the date when they are planned. I may decide today that, if it rains tomorrow, I will go to the restaurant for lunch and have a veal cutlet. If, when tomorrow comes, it does not rain and I decide not to go to the restaurant but to have a sandwich outside instead, I am not being inconsistent, since my plan to have a cutlet was contingent on the weather being bad. But if it does rain and I decide not to have the cutlet after all, I am not seeing the decision problem of what to eat that day at lunch from the same viewpoint. Technically this means I am not using the same utility function today compared to the one I used yesterday. Consequently, I am reneging on my plan, made yesterday, to have a veal cutlet if it rains. Such behavior is ruled out for individuals who have a unique utility function.

The economic approach of imposing restrictions on human behavior on the basis of methodological discipline has one big advantage and one big drawback. The big advantage is that these restrictions are by definition minimal, so that economic theory can be completely agnostic about what people like and what their motivations are. This stands in sharp contrast to lines of thought such as psychoanalysis, which not only postulates the existence of unconscious desires but also takes a stand on the content of those desires.

Of course, the less one is willing to assume about people's tastes and motivations, the lower the predictive content of the theory; hence the concern that the theory might be empty. It turns out, however, that despite such agnosticism, economic theory actually can be tested on the grounds of *some* predictions that solely derive from the assumptions that individuals rationally maximize their utility. Admittedly these predictions are scarce, but in principle there is always room for the theory to be specialized and to predict, for example, that if tastes have a given shape then prices will behave in a certain way. Should that prediction be rejected, this would simply mean that the restrictions made about preferences do not hold, not that the general foundations of economics are incorrect. By contrast, any proposition that violates the hypothesis of a unitary individual invalidates those general foundations.

The big disadvantage is that even the minimal assumptions on individual behavior upon which the theory rests can be invalidated, since they are not grounded on empirical evidence. What if we go out in the real world and find that some people do not have concave or transitive preferences after all? It is the realization of this shortcoming that has led to the rise of behavioral economics, discussed in the next chapter.

▌Government Intervention in Traditional Economics

Although economics is not very restrictive with respect to what one should observe, when it comes to policy prescriptions it implies a powerful presumption in favor of laissez-faire. Most important, the economic approach has scope for government intervention if there are market failures or redistributive concerns. But in both cases this intervention cannot be *paternalistic*; that is, there are no such things as desirable "social objectives" or "target outcomes" to be imposed on the people. Any "social goal" must be derived from the individuals' actual preferences.[1]

One important consequence of the view that individuals are unitary is that people act in their own interest. Therefore, their choices reveal their preferences, in the sense that if an alternative option is available, then the chosen option is necessarily superior to the alternative. Thus, if I decide to go to the ballet tonight instead of the restaurant, assuming either option is affordable, it must mean that the ballet gives me greater welfare than the restaurant. Any government policy that would distort my choice in favor of going to the restaurant is therefore inefficient in that it runs against my preferences. This is not only true for a policy that would force me to go to the restaurant rather than the ballet, if, for example, it prohibited ballets in the name of some ideology or social goal. It would also be true of a policy that would induce me to pick the restaurant rather than the ballet by subsidizing the former. In such a case my choice remains voluntary, but the inefficiency remains: it is just shifted to the taxpayer—if I had to pay the subsidy myself I would again pick the ballet over the restaurant.

Therefore, policy should not interfere with individual choice. If two individuals trade with each other, while each could decide not to, it must be that their transaction is mutually advantageous. Thus policy should not restrict trade. If somebody is given more opportunities, he always has the option of retaining his former decisions. Therefore, extending the set of available choices necessarily makes him better off. Consequently, policies that increase individual freedom (in that sense) are a priori good, and policies that restrict the set of choices are a priori bad.

individual freedom

This logic is called the "revealed preferences" principle. It states that the action actually taken by a rational individual must make him "happier" than any available alternative. In particular, since increasing the set of available alternatives cannot make people worse off, "money buys happiness": an increase in income will necessarily result in a higher utility level. The reason, again, is that every consumption basket that was available with less money remains available with more money, or, equivalently, that one always has the option of not using the additional money.

Because the assumptions made by economics about individual behavior put very little restrictions on the actual content of their preferences, many phe

---

[1] We leave it to part 2 to provide some precise definitions of paternalism.

that could at face value be interpreted as evidence of failure to be rational can, in fact, be reconciled with the standard economic framework.

An example is addiction. It is customary to invoke addiction as a rationale to ban or heavily tax the consumption of some goods (e.g., drugs, alcohol, gambling, and pornography). A casual argument is that such bans would help people avoid being trapped, and therefore are good for them. Nevertheless, that a good is addictive does not invalidate the conclusion that people's choices reveal their preferences and that restricting them necessarily makes them worse off. Indeed, if policy makers were consistent about taxing addictive goods, then they would also consider a tax on "good" addictions such as reading. While reading certainly is not hazardous to my health, it may have milder adverse consequences such as missing a train, a job interview, and the like. Yet any politician who would propose a tax on reading would be ridiculed. In fact, there is no proposal either to combat addiction to TV or videogames, although that may come.

The reason why state intervention to combat addictions is not granted is that an individual may be subject to addiction and yet remain unitary. At face value, that may sound like a paradox. If I develop an addiction, don't I have in some sense a different personality from what I would be if I had not started consuming the substance? The answer is that the individual's tastes evolve over time as a result of his past decisions, but that does not make his self multiple. The individual will still evaluate a given sequence of decisions in a unique way, irrespective of when and in what circumstances that evaluation takes place. Addiction means that the amount of welfare that I get from consuming a basket of goods in the future depends on my choices today. For example, I will like chocolate better tomorrow if I have chocolate today. And not having any chocolate tomorrow will make me feel miserable, more so the greater the quantity of chocolate I am having today. But when deciding how much chocolate to eat today, I rationally take into account that I will be addicted in the future. Suppose that once having recognized those effects, I nevertheless go ahead and have a lot of chocolate. I will subsequently suffer from this choice because of its addictive effects. Nevertheless, when making that decision, I decided that the immediate pleasure is greater than the future pain from addiction. When experiencing the pain, I do not regret my past decision. I would make it again if brought back to the past and faced with the same circumstances. In that sense, the individual remains unitary. His current suffering from addiction does not reflect inconsistent choices; it only reflects his own arbitrage in face of a trade-off.

As long as the individual remains unitary, the revealed preference principle applies and the decision to go ahead with the addictive behavior must make the individual better off than abstinence would.

It follows that the addictive nature of some goods provides no ground for specific government intervention. A similar argument applies to the view that

[2] See Becker and Murphy 1988.

compulsory pension schemes should be imposed because people "undersave." By "undersaving," people only reveal that they prefer to consume now rather than later. That this makes them poorer, and therefore less happy, in the future is no proof of inconsistency. Their relative poverty is simply the consequence of their own past rational choices, and they expected it when deciding to consume rather than save. Again, that they faced an intertemporal trade-off (i.e., a trade-off between consuming now versus tomorrow) should not be mistaken for a sign of inconsistent behavior. For unitary individuals, such trade-offs are no different from the intratemporal trade-offs such as that between going to the restaurant or the ballet.

did they really?

The revealed preference principle delivers a central theoretical result of economic science, the so-called first welfare theorem. It states that economic equilibrium is "optimal" in the sense that it leads to an allocation of resources such that no reallocation could make everybody better off. Such a situation is called a *Pareto optimum.* An allocation of resources that is not Pareto optimal is inefficient, in the sense that one could reallocate production and consumption in such a way that the utility of *all* individuals would go up.[3] Obviously, if that were so, there would be unanimous support for a government intervention that would coordinate society on the better outcome (called a *Pareto-improving* one).

Pareto

It is important to keep in mind that there are many Pareto optima. If my sister and I have to share a cake, any split that does not involve a waste of cake is a Pareto optimum: I cannot increase the amount of cake I eat without reducing the size of my sister's slice. Thus the competitive equilibrium is a Pareto optimum, but there are other Pareto optima that are equally efficient in that sense but that would not be reached through laissez-faire.

Why is the competitive equilibrium Pareto optimal? Revealed preferences play a key role in the intuition for this result. The idea is essentially that, because of revealed preferences, the only consumption baskets that could possibly make me better off are those that I cannot financially afford. Otherwise I would have bought them instead of the one I actually purchased. But then this means that in a Pareto-improving allocation, everybody must live beyond their means, which is not possible: if some people consume more than what they earn, others must subsidize them and consume less than what they earn.

If one believes in the first welfare theorem, then those who advocate government intervention must bear the burden of proof. They must provide an argument as to why the laissez-faire outcome is unsatisfactory. The two main arguments for intervention in traditional economics are redistributive concerns—the first welfare theorem holds, but one "dislikes" the allocation despite the fact that it is Pareto optimal, and would prefer another Pareto optimum instead—and market failures—the first welfare theorem fails because some of its assumptions are not valid.

2 arguments for intervention

---

[3] More precisely, it would either go up or stay constant, and strictly go up for at least one person.

▌ Fairness and Redistributive Concerns: Introducing the Social Welfare Function

One may justify government intervention on the premise that the outcome of competitive markets is "unfair"; that is, while the welfare of everybody could not be increased (by virtue of the first welfare theorem), the distribution of welfare among individuals is nevertheless considered inadequate and one is willing to reduce some people's welfare to increase that of others. A critical question is, of course, who is this "one" who does not like the laissez-faire outcome? Surely those who are supposed to be taxed by "one" prefer the laissez-faire to the allocation that "one" would like. The typical answer to that question lies in assuming the existence of a "social welfare function" that would represent the preferences of "society," just like the utility function describes the preferences of the individual. Such a "social welfare function" cannot be arbitrary; otherwise one could promote subsidies on the production of green beans on the grounds that consuming green beans is a "desirable social goal" regardless of whether people actually like them. Instead, the "social welfare function" must be based on individual preferences and should only tell us how they should be *aggregated* into a social objective. Minimally this means that the level of social welfare should go up if the welfare of all individuals go up. Therefore, if a situation is not Pareto optimal, a Pareto improvement must increase the social welfare level. From the social welfare function one may then derive society's preferred allocation of resources, best interpreted as that Pareto-optimal allocation that yields society's preferred distribution of welfare among individuals.[4] By contrast, a social welfare function that would not be an aggregate of individual welfare would not deliver a Pareto optimum; it would yield a preferred policy that is "paternalistic" in the sense that it imposes on the people an outcome that they do not "want," since there exists an alternative outcome that makes everybody better off, according to each one's own preferences.

Using traditional wording, I contend that the approach that consists of using a social welfare function which is an aggregate of individual utilities is "utilitarian." Every time I refer to utilitarianism, it means that some social planner tries to maximize such an aggregate, regardless of the specifics of how the aggregate is constructed.[5]

Consider the following example: John likes records, and Mary likes books. One record delivers to John exactly as many units of welfare as one book deliv-

---

[4] A simple representation of a social welfare function is a weighted sum of the utilities of all individuals. Each weight tells us the extent to which "society" cares about the welfare of the corresponding individual.

[5] Strictly speaking, utilitarianism means that one gives the same weight to each individual's utility, but I use that concept in a broader sense. In particular, I consider a Rawlsian social welfare function, which puts all the weight to the worst-off group in society, as just another variant of utilitarianism.

ers to Mary.[6] Each book costs $10, as does each record.[7] John is richer than Mary: he has $100, whereas she only has $60. Clearly, in a free market equilibrium, John will consume ten records and Mary six books. Assume now that there is an egalitarian social planner who does not like such an outcome. The social planner could achieve "equality" by taking five records away from John and giving them to Mary, while taking three books away from Mary and giving them to John. This would obviously be a stupid policy. First, it would be inefficient: books are produced using valuable resources, to be consumed by John who prefers records. Similarly, Mary ends up with records she does not want. Second, it is not actually egalitarian: John gets five records, but Mary only gets three books. In contrast, a utilitarian social planner will take into account that John prefers records and Mary prefers books. One way to achieve equality while respecting those preferences would be to take $20 away from John and give that money to Mary. In such a situation, each has $80. John buys eight books and Mary buys eight records. The welfare level is equalized between John and Mary. This is the outcome preferred by a social planner whose social welfare function gives equal weight to John and Mary.

Where Do Social Preferences Come From?

Assuming that social preferences are some aggregate of individual preferences obviously begs the question of where they come from. One could go back to Rousseau and introduce some abstract notion of "general will." That would amount to assuming some supra-individual being whose preferences supersedes that of people. Such an approach would put no restriction on the social welfare function, which could again be arbitrary and justify forcing people to eat green beans despite the fact that they hate them. It has proved more appealing for utilitarians to use the notion of a *veil of ignorance.* The idea is that when formulating an opinion about the desirability of social outcomes, people reason *as if* they did not know who they are. Therefore, they do not maximize their own preferences but some expected utility that reflects the likelihood that they might be somebody else. For example, John is happy with ten records, but he might as well have been Mary and not so happy with only five books. Assume that John considers that it is equally likely that he might have been Mary instead. Then under a veil of ignorance he will give an equal weight to his utility and Mary's. On that basis he will support the redistributive government policy outlined above. If Mary also considers that she might have been John with an

---

[6] More precisely, we are actually assuming that the utility of John when consuming x records is the same as that of Mary when consuming x books, and that this common utility function is concave.

[7] These monetary amounts indirectly capture the resource costs of producing those goods, given the available technologies.

equal probability, she will support the same conclusion. If people evaluate the probability of being born a given individual at the same level, there is a single utilitarian social welfare function that everybody would use to evaluate outcomes, as long as they put themselves under a veil of ignorance.

This utilitarian social welfare function provides justifications for redistributive policies if utility is concave. Recall that concavity means that an extra unit of consumption yields fewer additional units of welfare, the greater the initial level of consumption. As a consequence, richer people value one unit of consumption less than poorer ones. Therefore, if the social planner is adding the welfare of the rich with that of the poor, then transferring consumption from the rich to the poor would increase the total welfare. Under a veil-of-ignorance interpretation, this would mean that the "representative individual" is made better off because he gains more from redistribution if he is unlucky and poor than he loses if he is lucky and rich.

In a similar vein, concavity implies that individuals value insurance: they lose less by reducing their consumption in good times, when their consumption is high, than they gain by increasing consumption by the same amount in bad times, when their consumption is low. For this reason they are willing to pay a positive price to purchase fair insurance. Therefore, the veil of ignorance interprets redistribution as a form of insurance for the "representative individual" against his actual outcomes when he becomes a real person. Here we see that concavity is not only a useful device for proving results; it also has substantial implications for the content of public policies.

The veil-of-ignorance assumption has important shortcomings. Clearly individuals inherit all their genetic background and a good deal of their environmental background before being capable of critical thinking, not to mention expressing political choices. It is not clear in what situation the individual must be to evaluate outcomes under a veil of ignorance. Ideally that should be prior to his birth, but one cannot make choices if one does not exist! That leaves us with two logical possibilities.

First, one can view the social welfare function as the expected utility of some abstract individual who exists prior to the birth of any actual persons and is being "insured" by redistributive policies against the risk of being born in such and such circumstances. The veil-of-ignorance assumption is then somewhat paternalistic in that the government maximizes the utility of that abstract individual rather than actual ones. Note, however, that the outcome is not totally arbitrary since it is Pareto optimal for the actual individuals.

Second, the veil of ignorance may be interpreted as the wish that adult individuals have some degree of altruism by giving some weight to other people's welfare. But then there is no reason why they should be altruistic in the same way and share the same social welfare function. Furthermore, if social preferences are based on ethical rather than logical considerations, how much weight should serial killers, or Adolf Hitler, get? Finally, even assuming that the veil of ignorance is perfect in that all individuals entirely ignore who they really are and maximize the same welfare function, one must still take a stand on how individual preferences are aggregated. Specifically, for example, how much does "society" dislike the risk of being in a disadvantageous situation? In his *Theory of Justice*, Rawls (1971) proposes that society should infinitely dislike being in that situation. In other words, the social welfare function should be reduced to the utility of the individuals who are worst off. In terms of the above model, that would mean that society only cares about Mary's welfare if she consumes less than John, and vice versa.[8] This assumption, called the *maximin principle,* is added to that of a veil of ignorance, and leads to supporting as much redistribution as possible given the constraints imposed by markets and incentives. But it is quite arbitrary, indeed very "European," and one may as well consider a more "American" social welfare function where (under the same veil of ignorance) people value the prospect of being successful and give far greater weight to the most successful individuals than Rawls advocates.

Despite its imperfections, the social welfare function has the merit of putting serious limits on the kinds of government policies that are acceptable. This is because the only acceptable social welfare functions must be aggregates of individual preferences. In the above example, forcing John and Mary to consume five records and three books each is an unacceptable government policy, as it runs against individual preferences. Under a veil of ignorance, John would like Mary to be richer than under the laissez-faire outcome, but he certainly would not like her to listen to records instead of reading books. An important implication is that government intervention cannot be paternalistic, in that it cannot prescribe the actions of individuals. All it can do is change their overall opportunities by redistributing *income* between them; that is, *conditional* on redistributing income, one should again opt for laissez-faire. This conclusion is summarized by the "second welfare theorem." This result says that any Pareto-optimal allocation—and particularly the one that maximizes the social welfare function—can be obtained as a market equilibrium provided one has put in place a set of redistributive transfers between the individuals. As illustrated in our example above, a tax on John's income which is rebated to Mary, and equalizes their post-tax, post-transfer income, would implement the preferred allocation for a social welfare function with equal weights. The free operation of markets then guarantees that the productive resources are correctly allocated between books and records, and that these goods are correctly allocated between John and Mary.[9]

---

[8] In that simple context, the Rawlsian social welfare function leads to the same prescription that John's and Mary's welfare should be equalized.

[9] An important aspect of the Second Welfare Theorem is that equilibrium market prices reflect the true *social* value of alternative activities. In other words, the price of a tomato relative to bananas is equal to how many bananas the social planner is willing to sacrifice in order to produce one tomato; if a small amount of bananas are transformed into tomatoes at that rate, that leaves the value of the social welfare function unchanged.

Externalities and Market Failures

The other main scope for government intervention is that markets do not work as well as postulated in the first welfare theorem. One main source of market failure is the existence of *externalities*, that is, interactions between individuals that are not mediated by market prices. The archetypal example is pollution: since there are no property rights on air, polluters are not charged for the costs they impose on others—they do not have to purchase the air they are polluting. As a result there is too much pollution, and that leaves room for the government to intervene by taxing polluting activities.

The existence of externalities is in some sense a rationale for more government intrusion in private affairs than redistributive concerns. This is because, rather than redistributing income, the government now wants to change prices. If markets are competitive and there are no externalities, prices are "correct" in that they reflect the true costs of producing a good (as well as the true value of consuming it). For example, the price of a car reflects the value of the time of the workers involved in the production process, plus the value of the materials that have been used, and so on. If there are externalities, market prices no longer reflect the true social costs and benefits of alternative activities. For example, if I contribute to road congestion when I take my car on the road, that is an externality. It is then optimal to impose some tax on the use of one's car (for example, by levying an excise tax on gasoline). Such a tax is called a *Pigovian tax*, named after British economist A. C. Pigou.[10] In principle, the Pigovian tax should be equal to the monetary equivalent of the loss of time I impose on others by increasing road congestion. If the tax is correctly computed, then the level of congestion will be optimally determined.

Correctly charging for an externality implies a complicated process of calculation. For example, to evaluate the cost to society of road congestion, the government must measure private preferences. It can no longer rely on markets to reveal them. The market price of a car will tell me how much drivers value road transportation, but it will not tell me how miserable those who are stuck in traffic jams feel. To measure that quantity, I have to conduct a survey.

Nevertheless, externalities do not justify arbitrary government intervention, much less those grounded on paternalistic motives. Economics does not tell us, for example, that because cars cause congestion, they should be eliminated. It tells us that the welfare loss of congestion should be properly measured so that it can be properly charged. It may well turn out that the estimated damage is minor so that the optimal tax should be small. The government should not presume the outcome of such a measurement process. It is highly unlikely, in fact, that a given activity should be banned altogether. Such a ban is equivalent to an infinite tax and imposes very large losses on those individuals who especially value the activity. On those grounds, many real-world policies can be challenged

---

[10] See Pigou 1920.

as too interventionist, such as the one child policy in China, banning drugs or alcohol, and so forth.   *missing markets → externalities*

Furthermore, economists have realized that the ultimate reason for externalities is *missing markets.* Under that view, government intervention is a second-best fix for the fact that there are things on which one cannot trade. This suggests that one may consider developing markets as an alternative to taxation. Returning to the congestion example, if roads were private, then the owner of the road would take into account that people would be willing to pay less to use his road if they expect it to be congested, and charge a price reflecting the congestion externality.[11] Of course, the reason why a market may be missing may also be deep. Creating a market uses resources.[12] Space constraints limit the number of alternative roads that connect two given points with each other. And it is not practical to set up many tolls for drivers. Nevertheless, creating new markets sometimes works and that allows the government to be "blinder" and refrain from taxation. One example is the market for SO_2 emissions in the United States, which is an efficient substitute for uniform emission standards.[13]

▍ Responsibility in Economics: The Role of Imperfect Information and Moral Hazard

Moral Hazard

As one moves further away from the assumptions underlying the welfare theorems, the bases for limited government become shakier. The result that an *optimal* allocation, reflecting the redistributive concerns of "society," can be decentralized by using a simple system of transfers, breaks down if there are informational problems in observing individual actions—a phenomenon we usually call *moral hazard.*[14] Optimal government intervention, then, should be more complex and typically rely on more instruments; that is, it should be more *intrusive.*

---

[11] Thus the theory of clubs states that if externalities are local, they can be solved by clubs that charge an entry fee and have property rights on the resources that is subject to the externality. See Tiebout 1956 and Ellickson et al. 1999 for a modern treatment of general equilibrium with clubs and free entry.

[12] See De Meza and Gould 1992.

[13] Note that there is no economic result that tells us that creating a market is preferable to imposing a Pigovian tax. Nor does the latter a priori reduce freedom more than a trading scheme, since the former forces firms to acquire permits to undertake production. In fact, in the absence of informational frictions, Pigovian taxation and creating markets are equivalent. See Weitzman 1974 for a related discussion on price instruments versus quantity instruments.

[14] Another, totally different argument is that people may be *misinformed.* For example, somebody may try drugs while not aware of its addictive effects. It is then too late to unravel that decision when feeling the pain of addiction. It is beyond the scope of this book to discuss that argument, but let us note that, at best, it justifies government provision of information rather than government intrusion in private transactions, and that one has to make the case that governments are better than markets and families at providing information.

In the theoretical situation where the second welfare theorem applies, a government with distributive concerns knows who would get "too much" and who would get too little if it abstained from intervening. For this reason it can "correct" the free-market allocation by transferring money between people *irrespective of their actions*. Arguably such a system involves as little intrusion as possible, given the government redistributive goal. It is also neutral from the point of view of individual responsibility: the transfer to which each individual is entitled depends on his birth characteristics (supposedly observable by the government, and from which the government is supposed to infer the utility level that the individual can hope for) but is independent of its actions. Therefore the transfers do not reward good actions and do not penalize bad actions; but nor do they do the opposite.

If individual characteristics (such as talent, taste for work, and so forth) are unobservable, the government, if it wants to redistribute between individuals, must base its transfers upon *outcomes* rather than characteristics.[15] If outcomes are themselves the result of unobservable individual actions, then redistributive policies are faced with a moral hazard problem. This means that the "social planner" must choose between a more intrusive design of the transfer system vs. rewarding irresponsibility.[16]

The most salient moral hazard problem for redistributive policies is that we want to discourage people from voluntarily putting themselves in positions where they would become a burden on the welfare state. We know, for example, that drug addicts are more likely to become dependent on welfare and that old people without their own savings will fall on some assistance scheme. The argument goes, therefore, that these individuals are exerting some "externality" on the public budget and compulsory pension plans, or a ban on drugs can be thought of as a way to correct these externalities. Here people are not harming themselves but are harming others who have to pay for their deeds. That is the justification for imposing restrictions on individual behavior.

That argument not only presupposes the existence of a welfare state (as opposed to, say, voluntary private insurance schemes), but it also assumes that the welfare state cannot discriminate between an individual being in a poor situation out of his own making and someone having suffered from truly adverse shocks. But such discrimination is efficient as long as society considers individuals as unitary. It is the logic that prevails when the unemployment insurance system compensates workers for involuntary job losses but not for quitting their job. It is not clear why one should not apply the same logic to people who end up in trouble out of their own past consumption choices. (Conditioning eligibility on past choices is also justified in some traditional moral sense, since individuals who put themselves in welfare dependency out of their own making can only "blame themselves.")

---

[15] It is also possible that characteristics are observed but that some ethical principle precludes using them as a basis for redistribution. See the discussion on screening in chapter 8.

[16] A standard reference here is Mirrlees 1971.

In fact, standard utilitarian economics[17] has extensively studied the moral hazard issue associated with the welfare state in a branch of the literature which we may call "dynamic social contracting theory." This research says that to mitigate the moral hazard problem one should condition current redistribution to the whole history of the individual's past outcomes, so as to give that individual the strongest possible incentives to undertake the right actions. This implies imposing high future penalties for inappropriate behavior today; thus, for example, having saved too little today would typically reduce one's future claims to welfare, everything else equal. The reason is that if individuals are unitary, they will properly take into account the adverse consequences that some choices today will have on their future welfare eligibility.[18]

Dynamic social contract theory does not validate the idea that individuals forcing themselves into welfare dependency is a major issue—if they do so, they will experience large penalties. On the other hand, there is already a paternalistic dimension in conditioning transfers on past actions, since it amounts to an implicit system of taxes and subsidies on those actions, and authorities have to keep track of them.[19] For example, a penalty imposed on individuals who saved too little is not very far from a paternalistic scheme that would force people to save a minimum fraction of their income. But it is improving on it in that it recognizes that current needs may be high—or that some people may prefer to consume a lot now and little later—and it leaves current decisions to the individual provided he accepts that those decisions will condition his future welfare

[17] See, for example, Atkeson and Lucas 1992; Farhi and Werning 2005; and Grochulski and Kocherlakota 2007.

[18] This point is studied in a paper by Atkeson and Lucas 1992. They consider a world where people are sometimes "needy" and should consume more when they are in such a situation. If the government could directly observe whether people are needy it would just redistribute money to them. The problem is that everybody then would have an incentive to claim that they are "needy" and would do so if that condition were not directly observable. The authors show that the optimal social contract involves redistributing in favor of the needy in exchange for a permanent reduction in their subsequent utility, implemented through a permanent reduction in their claims to the welfare state. Although the setup is somewhat abstract, this can be interpreted as a welfare state that would redistribute less to those that have saved less in the past, where saving less is indeed some signal of past needs. In their model, the unluckiest individuals—those who have experienced a sequence of bad shocks—become poorer and poorer and inequality widens over time. Tolerating these bad outcomes is optimal, because they are discounted by their low probability in the representative individual's evaluation of his welfare and their counterpart is that the moral hazard problem is solved, which means that effort and productivity are high and so is the amount of money that can be redistributed. Thus a perfectly utilitarian social planner can tolerate huge inequalities in the future because these are inequalities between consumption levels of the *same* individual under alternative sequences of shocks, and this individual naturally aggregates them under a veil of ignorance.

[19] A typical example in the moral hazard literature is the imposition of a tax on layoffs when there is an unemployment benefit system; the moral hazard problem is that firms and workers will excessively rely on unemployment benefits since these are paid by a third party. Thus the optimal contract involves a feature akin to the U.S. "experience rating" system which increases employers' contributions whenever they have a history of laying off too many people. See Feldstein 1976; and Blanchard and Tirole 2008.

entitlements. Absent moral hazard, however, the optimal redistributive scheme would not be conditional on the past history of shocks and therefore would be less intrusive.

This said, in the debate on moral hazard many advocate for even more intervention than predicted by the dynamic social contracting approach, and this despite that modern welfare states often do not hold individuals accountable for their past choices: eligibility to assistance income, in most countries where it exists, is unconditional. People who engage in hazardous behavior enjoy the same public health coverage as others. Rather than having them take into account the consequences of their actions, the government directly penalizes them by taxing and banning smoking or imposing compulsory participation in public pensions. One reason is, of course, that individuals are not treated as unitary, to which we return in the rest of the book. Another is that the state itself is not a unitary individual and cannot enforce its own commitment to punish those who saved too little. This is the political economy critique discussed below.

Notable here is that utilitarianism is "morally neutral"—it does not embody any "value" other than as defined by the individuals' utility functions—which reinforces the tendency for the welfare state to be "weak," namely, to renege on its commitments and fail to punish the undersavers. The reason is that the only value of such a punishment is to deter undersaving in the first place: dynamic social contracting theory tells us that the *prospect* of being poor in the future should be used as an instrument to elicit proper incentives *now*. But once the future has arrived, enforcing the penalty no longer has any incentive virtue since the relevant actions have already been undertaken. In other words, it is the *expectation* of a weak government that is distortionary, not that the government is weak at a given point in time. For example, the government may decide to extend some benefit to social groups that should not be eligible, given their past record, considering the political benefits of such a measure and that no inefficiency is being created at the time it is undertaken. Things would be different if instead of being purely utilitarian, social values reflected some moral imperative stating that improvidence should not be condoned. A weak government would then violate such an imperative; therefore, incentives for governments to be weak would be lower.[20] On the other hand, the purely utilitarian government may implement paternalistic policies that preclude the undesired action in order to solve its own commitment problem.

Yet it is interesting to note that revealed preferences provide foundations for the view that it is morally acceptable to deny benefits to people who end up on welfare out of their own choices. The argument is as follows. By revealed preference, somebody who is in need because of his own past choices cannot be worse off than if alternative choices had been made. Therefore he does not deserve

[20] A related issue, beyond the scope of this book, is how such moral values have evolved, as they indirectly provide society with commitment technologies that enhance its reproductive success in the long run.

public support more than anybody who was initially in the same situation but has made different choices. By that metric it is even immoral to tax a minimum wage earner to support, say, a person who was originally wealthier but became indigent because of some addiction such as drugs. In other words, individuals receiving welfare must be compared not at a point in time but in an intertemporal fashion. Those who are poorer now because they saved less in the past enjoyed a greater consumption in the past; thus they are not worse off in terms of their total intertemporal flow of utility compared to those who made thriftier choices.[21]

The Worm Is in the Fruit

The two welfare theorems apparently provide economic and philosophical foundations for a "liberal" society where "collective" welfare is reconciled with individual welfare, since the former is defined as a particular way to aggregate the latter, and since it can be reached by using instruments that are as unintrusive as possible. As the preceding discussion of moral hazard suggests, these foundations are shaky. We now further discuss why.

First, let us reconsider the second welfare theorem. It states that the best "socially desirable" outcome may be reached by redistributing income appropriately and then let markets operate freely. Typically the economist then thinks of himself as an agent who does not formulate a judgment on social objectives but instead sets the best instruments so as to attain these objectives efficiently. But this becomes a slippery slope whenever there is some confusion as to what precisely is a legitimate objective. As far as redistribution is concerned, the economic approach only allows for "society" to give more or less weight to the welfare of an individual, depending, say, on his relative status. In particular, social objectives should *not* be specified in terms of targets imposed from above without regard to what people truly want. In principle, "reducing poverty by x percent" need not be a legitimate social goal from the point of view of economics,

---

[21] The argument I have just spelled out also seems valid from a purely utilitarian perspective, since one may argue that richer people have a lower marginal utility of wealth than poorer people, regardless of how the money is used. Thus an initially richer person who ends up on welfare because of poor past choices has a lower marginal utility of wealth than an initially poorer person, which justifies redistributing in favor of the latter rather than the former. This argument, however, is in fact fallacious because the two individuals must have a different utility function in order for the initially richer person to end up with a lower consumption level so that they may be aggregated in the social welfare function in such a way that the richer person has a higher marginal utility, which means that he is more "eager" to consume than the other. This, of course, ignores the conceptual difficulty in making interpersonal comparisons of utility, but such difficulty must be disregarded if one is to use a utilitarian social welfare function. A similar difficulty arises if one wishes to distinguish an individual who spends a lot because he is "needy" from one who does so because he is "greedy." Although the two terms convey different moral connotations, they both mean the same thing in terms of utility, namely, that one wants to consume a lot now relative to the future.

because it may be (for some definition of poverty) that no Pareto optimum satisfies that requirement. In such a situation, the economist cannot take the social objective as granted but instead must point out that it is incompatible with efficiency. In practice, it is easier to specify objectives in terms of target outcomes than in terms of some abstract-looking social welfare function. And, when the issue is just redistribution, it is likely that most plausible objectives can be associated with some implicit social welfare function—although the problem remains that if there are several "desirable social goals," they may correspond to different sets of individual weights, meaning that social preferences are inconsistent. But the confusion between social preferences and social outcomes may become more acute when it applies to the other rationale for intervention— externalities. It is often tempting, in such a case, to reinterpret tautologically any target outcome as an externality, which validates it and confines the economist to the role of computing the optimal Pigovian tax that enforces the "social objective." For example, there is wide agreement in Western circles that female labor market participation should be increased,[22] and yet there is nothing that tells us that it is inefficiently low a priori.[23] What if, after all, women want to work less than men do? The social objective would then lead to an inefficient (i.e., non–Pareto-optimal) allocation of time between market work, home production, and leisure. Yet many economists would not question its efficiency and would simply propose their preferred instrument for attaining it.[24]

Although these confusions are dangerous since they may validate any kind of intervention, they may in principle be avoided by a careful intellectual discipline. Of greater importance is the fundamental philosophical flaw of the economic approach that it does not value individual freedom per se. Laissez-faire is just an instrument that allows us to use decentralized information so as to attain efficiency. To an economist, individual freedom is worth what the theorems are worth. Relaxing the assumptions upon which the theorems are built undermines the presumption in favor of laissez-faire. Economics does not consider that there is a human right to property or to participate in markets. Even John Stuart Mill, acting in the capacity of political philosopher, claims to base his defense of liberty on utilitarian considerations only:

> It is proper to state that I forego any advantage which could be derived to my argument from the idea of abstract right, as a thing independent of

[22] The reader may scroll through any report by the Organisation for Economic Co-operation and Development (OECD) or the World Bank, or read the famous "Lisbon Agenda" of the European Union.

[23] An ongoing debate concerns whether women earn less because they are discriminated against or whether the income gap is a measurement issue or the result of women's own choices. We do not discuss this here; the simple point is that policy should not presume, a priori, what an optimal outcome looks like. If one group of people have different preferences, then their outcomes should look different even at the "social" optimum.

[24] A more subtle approach is to develop a theory where some market failure is introduced that validates the target outcome. In many cases, however, the best policy predicted by the theory differs from setting the target outcome. It is just that the target outcome does better than no policy at all.

utility. *I regard utility as the ultimate appeal on all ethical questions;* but it must be utility in the largest sense, grounded on the permanent interests of man as a progressive being.[25]

Later in his book, *On Liberty*, Mill spells out some utilitarian arguments in favor of individual freedom. It leads to a greater diversity of individual actions which by virtue of example are conducive to innovation and societal progress; people are better informed about their own interests than are others; and so forth.

For economic science, markets and competition are simply a computer that yields an optimal resource allocation thanks to the invisible hand—just as natural selection, in biology, allows Nature to replicate a computer seeking to optimize organisms. A famous controversy arose in the 1930s between Hayek (following Mises) and Oskar Lange over centrally planned economies.[26] Hayek argued that central planning could not possibly reach an efficient allocation of resources because of the incentive problems and the enormous amount of information that needed to be collected. Lange's answer was that in a centrally planned economy the government could simply act so as to *replicate* the operation of markets, by sending price signals to individuals and firms, and adjusting them iteratively to correct imbalances between supply and demand, so as to reach an equilibrium. This would achieve efficiency while doing away with the need for private property and private contracts. Obviously such a solution was totally impractical at that time. But it is disturbing that the argument in favor of contractual freedom boils down to its practical virtues; in fact, that argument may quickly fade as new information technologies may one day make Lange's central planning system workable. The economic case for laissez-faire would then be completely dead.[27] Indeed, people's movements can be tracked using their mobile phones; their conversations can be recorded. Their electricity consumption can be measured in real time by modern sophisticated meters. Their actions in the street can be filmed by CCTV. Their car trips are filmed by radars, and, in the United Kingdom, it was recently proposed that a computer chip be installed in cars so that each car could be tracked at any point in time, with numerous applications from better elicitation of crime to optimal traffic regulation to perfect enforcement of speed limits.

Another illustration of that point is the economic theory of optimal taxation. The only limits to taxation that this theory considers are those that result from the *distortionary* effects of taxes. In other words, the only reason one should be reluctant to tax labor income is that it discourages work and thus reduces the total labor input into production. Similarly, capital income taxation reduces

[25] See Mill 1863.

[26] See Lange 1936; Hayek 1937, 1940; and Mises 1920.

[27] In fairness to Hayek, however, let us point out that he was fighting on both fronts and also defended freedom on intrinsic grounds. In *The Road to Serfdom* (1944), he writes: "Liberalism [...] regards competition as superior not only because in most circumstances it is the most efficient method known but because it is the only method which does not require the coercive or arbitrary intervention of authority."

the incentives for productive investment and should therefore be limited. Most economists, if faced with a putative economy where such distortions do not exist, would advocate for a 100 percent tax rate. This is because the only costs of taxation, in an economic model, are the distortions; if the labor income tax can be increased while ensuring that people work just as hard as before, then economists would recommend such an intervention, since there is no loss of production and the tax receipts can be used to implement policies that enhance welfare. There is no principle in economics stating that it is "wrong" for the government to expropriate people. Notably surveys show that the more inelastic are the actions being taxed, that is, the more efficient the tax is from an economic viewpoint, the more likely the taxes are considered unfair. This is presumably because people value freedom, and such taxes make them feel trapped and exploited.

The deeper reason why economics does not value freedom per se but only as a means to an end is that economics is _consequentialist_.[28] Consequentialism means that, in the system of thought we are considering, the value of an action—or, in the case of most interest to us, a policy—only depends on the final consequences of that action. Therefore, two policies that have the same effect on the allocation of resources are, by definition, equivalent. This is only natural to an economist who seeks to maximize a social welfare function where the instruments used to achieve a maximum do not enter in the social welfare function, and only the final allocation does. An apt example is a tax called Contribution Sociale Généralisée (CSG), which was introduced in France in the early 1990s. That tax was withheld on workers' pay; when filing their income tax return, people have to declare not their post-CSG income but their pre-CSG income. In other words, they have to declare a sum which is larger that the sum they actually earned. Two economists rightly pointed out in the press that it does not matter, as that system is equivalent to a system where one declares the lower post-CSG income, but the income tax rate is higher. That people are taxed on money which in fact they did not earn is irrelevant to an economist; all that matters is how much they consume at the end of the day.

A natural corollary of consequentialism is that one only cares about the allocation of resources at the end, not about the process by which resources were allocated. That is why the libertarians who often fall in the trap of consequentialism, by criticizing a policy measure not on the grounds that it violates some fundamental freedom but because it would not work, make a big mistake. For a consequentialist, the taxable CSG is the same as the nontaxable one. Lange's authoritarian method for allocating resources is as respectable as Hayek's, which relies on free will and self-interest. And if all Hayek has to say about Lange's proposal is that it is impractical, the outlook for free will is bleak.

Once the premises of consequentialism are accepted, we can only object to some government intervention on _instrumental_ grounds, by questioning its

---

[28] This is akin to Nozick's notion of an "end-state view."

feasibility or its costs, or by pointing to unintended consequences. This stands in contrast to *principled* objections, which state that the intervention violates some fundamental principle upon which society is built.[29] Although such principles may be logical or philosophical, they will quite often be ethical. The economic case for laissez-faire is purely instrumental and does not resort to any ethical argument. There is great beauty in this attempt to base limited government on a scientific prescription. Unfortunately, as I document below, it is crumbling under the progresses of that very science.

▌ Political Economy

The most viable consequentialist critique of government is the one economists refer to as "political economy." Utilitarian prescriptions for government intervention, whether aimed at correcting inequality or externalities, consider the state as an abstract benevolent entity whose only purpose is to maximize the social welfare function. The political economy critique instead realizes that the state is a coalition of real people who are equally self-interested. Instead of maximization of social welfare, policy is determined by interest groups, rent-seeking, and redistribution in favor of powerful lobbies and political majorities.[30] Political economy, then, asks how, in order to improve those nasty outcomes, the actions of the state may be constrained by some constitution. The constitution is presumably designed by altruistic Founding Fathers who presumably internalize social welfare. Thus political economy is utilitarian but recognizes the problems that "society" has in controlling the government's actions. Where the preferences of the Founding Fathers come from is again an unanswered question, but at least the political economy approach addresses the fallacy of considering the government, unlike the rest of society, as a god-like benevolent abstract entity, with the not-so-surprising result that governments can improve on markets since they maximize what society is supposed to maximize.

Political economy challenges both the view that the government seeks to maximize a social welfare function and the view that it is capable of rationally maximizing an objective in the same fashion as a unitary individual. Because the government is made of multiple people with conflicting interests, its behavior cannot generally be represented by a consistent social utility function.[31] In cases where that is possible, the resulting objective function delivered by the voting process has no particular reason to resemble the utilitarian's social

---

[29] For a discussion of principled versus consequentialist foundations of liberalism, see Rasmussen and Den Uyl 2005.

[30] The interested reader may refer to Persson and Tabellini 2000; Drazen 2001; and Alesina, Cohen, and Roubini 1997.

[31] That is the essence of the Condorcet paradox and the Arrow impossibility theorem which state that there is no voting procedure that aggregates individual preferences into consistent collective ones. See Arrow 1963 [1951].

welfare function. It will, instead, reflect the relative power of conflicting interest groups.

Because political economy shares the basic premises of utilitarianism, it does not value freedom per se. It simply is a practical statement that we live in a second-best world where one cannot make naive policy prescriptions irrespective of the political process, and that a more careful design must be considered. Political economy considerations may sometimes lead to a prescription for more freedom and sometimes less. For example, if we expect people who have not saved enough to organize themselves into a lobby supporting a transfer in favor of themselves, we may recommend that people are forced to save a minimum fraction of their income in order to prevent such future political undertakings.[32] In this example, the government has a behavioral problem which is the result of its inadequate political institutions that make such lobbying games possible. To solve that problem, which makes the state unable to commit to future policies, we recommend more restrictions on freedom than what a simple utilitarian would do if those political economy issues were ignored.

---

[32] In fact, there may be constitutional alternatives to such a prescription that one should carefully consider. But from a consequentialist perspective, such alternatives have no particular virtue compared to more direct interventions, and should be judged only according to the efficiency of the allocations they deliver.

4

Economics Goes Behavioral

In recent years economic theory has moved away from its foundations based on
the assumptions of rational individuals and on the central role of revealed preferences. The driving forces behind that evolution are threefold. First, the unitary paradigm appeared inconsistent with some empirical regularities of human
behavior. Second, and relatedly, there was dissatisfaction with the methodological rather than empirical basis for economics' depiction of individual choices;
it makes sense to construct economic theory on what students of individual
behavior—psychologists—have uncovered rather than on the modeler's intro-
spection. Third, the standard paradigm was getting close to exhaustion in terms
of its research potential, and there are high academic rewards to exploring novel
directions.

Most of the recent developments in behavioral economics converge with
other social sciences in that they do away with the unitary individual. To date,
behavioral economics is a catalogue of empirically documented psychological
phenomena, each a particular deviation from the unitary view. No attempt is
made to bring them together in a synthetic theory, nor to impose restrictions
on their frequency in the population. Although the unitary view imposes restrictions on preferences, these only imply some general properties that these
preferences must have in order to generate consistent behavior. Although Jennifer must prefer onions to chives if she favors onions over garlic and garlic over
chives, the theory does not tell us that onions are generally preferred over garlic. John, unlike Jennifer, may well prefer garlic over onions, as long as his preferences meet the same consistency requirements. The pro–laissez-faire results
rely on the virtues of voluntary exchange irrespective of the individuals' actual
preferences. Some people may prefer onions, others garlic. Some may be eager
to consume now, others later. Some may like to work hard, others may be lazy.
Economics accommodates diversity of behavior and does not apply any "general psychological law."[1]

---

[1] Keynes considered his General Theory to rest on the "fundamental psychological law" that
the propensity to consume was falling with income. But it was easily shown thereafter that such a
"law" was not necessary for the theory, in addition to being empirically dubious. See my brief discussion about the specialization of preferences in chapter 3.

On the other hand, behavioral economics makes statements about how people actually behave in the real world; specifically it documents *general* tendencies to deviate from rationality in a precise direction. It is disturbingly silent about how general these tendencies are. What if some people do not have them? That consideration should at least lead us to be cautious in deriving recommendations in favor of paternalistic policies from these psychological assumptions. Though many behavioral economists are indeed cautious, the thrust of this book is that behavioral economics inevitably contributes to the trend toward greater government intrusion that the demise of the unitary individual has facilitated. To understand that, let us discuss a number of the general psychological phenomena that are used by the research on behavioral economics.

These phenomena fall under several different headings, but their most salient aspect, for our purpose, is that in many (but not all) cases individuals are reinterpreted as having several "incarnations" rather than consisting of a unique self.

▎ Cognitive Dissonance → ppl process info incorrectly

Standard theory says that people should use all available information in order to make their best possible inference about the parameters that are relevant for their decisions. But it has been observed that people often process information so as to validate their past choices, that is, they give less weight, or even discard, signals which reveal that such choices might have been erroneous. That phenomenon is called *cognitive dissonance*. As an illustration, Lord, Ross, and Lepper (1979) performed an experiment in which they divide a pool of graduate students into two groups based on their answers to a preliminary questionnaire: Group I favors the death penalty because they believe it works; Group II opposes it and does not believe it works. The students are then asked to read academic studies on the efficacy of the death penalty and to report how reading these studies affected their beliefs. Both groups read the *same* set of studies. The authors find that Group I is more in favor of the death penalty than before reading the studies, and Group II is more against it. Thus people use new information in a biased way so as to confirm their prior beliefs.

Another form of cognitive dissonance is the "availability bias," by which people tend to give excessive weight to their own experience. Thus people who were mugged in a particular neighborhood will infer that it is generally a dangerous area, whereas those who were not will believe that this very same neighborhood is quite safe.

The availability bias may emerge in a more sophisticated manner when examined with quantitative evidence and statistics. Kahneman and Tversky (1971, 1972) demonstrated, in experiments they ran, that people did not properly understand the errors associated with some samples, thus revealing that they were too confident in using past statistical regularities to predict the future. Furthermore, rather than ascribing the events that were not predicted by their model to their estimated parameters' sampling error, they rationalized those outliers by finding some extraneous causal explanation.

Cognitive dissonance does not mean that the individual is not unitary. It just means that he does not have the perfect ability to process information that is usually assumed by economic models. However, as we shall see in the next chapter, in some instances that shortcoming comes close to having a non-unitary individual to the extent that his processing of information will lead him to disagree with policies that are supposed to enhance his welfare. In other words, one can interpret an individual who processes information incorrectly as having two incarnations: a self whose utility is maximized and a self who makes decisions.

Time Inconsistency

Much attention has been given to the phenomenon of time inconsistency. It is perhaps the most compelling example of multiple incarnations. The idea is that people evaluate different alternatives depending on the date on which they make their choice. This is not the case for a unitary individual, whose preferences do not depend on the time at which decisions are made. A unitary individual does not renege on his plans nor does he regret his choices, unless new information has arrived. For example, if in May I elect to go to graduate school next year rather accept that job offer, when September comes I will carry on with this plan. If I change my mind—the economy, say, is stronger than expected—that does not mean I am reneging on my plan: it simply means that my plan was (at least implicitly) contingent on the state of the economy, which turns out not to be what I had thought. Therefore, even though the outcome is not what I expected, I am implementing my plan. On the other hand, if I change my mind and finally accept the job offer despite the fact that no news has arrived, I am not behaving like a unitary individual. Instead, I am being time inconsistent: my preferences in September are different from my preferences in May.[2] Technically we may view that situation as the individual having a different incarnation every period. Each incarnation uses a different utility function so that its choices contradict those made by other incarnations.

A particularly important aspect of preferences is how people value consuming now versus in the future; a key component of the debate on government intervention has to do with the desirability and design of compulsory pension

---

[2] I abstract from the issue that in May I may just have been undecided, so that my "decision" was, in fact, just a working hypothesis. In such a case the individual may again be unitary but have long decision delays.

systems. Whether people are time consistent in their consumption choices has an important consequence for the answers economists would give to those questions.

The weight individuals give to present versus future streams of utility is captured by a parameter called the *subjective discount rate.* For intertemporal choice to be consistent, this discount rate should again not depend on the date at which decisions are made. Suppose, for example, I am willing to reduce my consumption by $100 in 2010, provided I can increase it by $104 in 2011. This means that my subjective discount rate between these two dates is 4 percent. I am then willing to sign a contract which stipulates that I pay $100 in 2010 and receive $104 in 2011. Time consistency then means that if I am willing to sign such a contract in 2009, I am also willing to sign it in 2010.

When people are time inconsistent, the subjective discount rate between two dates may depend on the date at which decisions are made. This means that I may agree in 2009 to invest my money in 2010 in exchange for a 4 percent return in 2011 but if that same decision has to be made in 2010, I may now require 6 percent: my subjective discount rate now depends on the date at which the investment decision is contemplated. More specifically, economists talk of *hyperbolic discounting*[3] whenever the subjective discount rate goes up as one approaches the date at which the investment has to be made. In other words, people value consumption at a given date relative to a later date more, the closer they are to the first date.

ppl want to consume now rather than later

Table 4.1 illustrates this property. I consider an individual who decides how much to consume at three different dates, denoted by t = 1, 2, 3. At date 1 the individual has to make a plan for consumption in this period and the next two periods, but at date 2 he may well reconsider that plan. The numbers in the table give us the amount of utility an individual obtains from consuming one unit of consumption. The columns define the date at which consumption takes place. The rows define the date at which the individual evaluates his utility. For example, the number 0.5 in row 1, column 2, tells us that, from the viewpoint of the individual at date 1, one unit of the good consumed at date 2 is worth 0.5 units of welfare.

Table 4.1. The Valuation of Consumption as a Function of the Date of Consumption and the Date on Which Utility Is Being Evaluated

	t = 1	t = 2	t = 3
t = 1	1	0.5	0.25
t = 2		1	0.5
t = 3			1

[3] This psychological phenomenon was uncovered by Chung and Herrnstein (1967). It came back into fashion in economics in particular with the work of Laibson (1997).

Table 4.1 shows that, if evaluated at $t = 1$, a dollar consumed at $t = 3$ is worth $0.25/0.5 = 0.5$ dollars consumed at $t = 2$. If I now evaluate this trade-off from the point of view of $t = 2$, I will consider that a dollar at $t = 3$ is worth $0.5/1 = 0.5$ dollars consumed at $t = 2$. Therefore, the arbitrage between consuming at $t = 3$ and consuming at $t = 2$ is independent of the date at which that choice is being considered. The individual has a single incarnation, whose preferences are defined by the first line of Table 4.1. The second and third lines are just what remains of these same preferences once one and two periods have elapsed, respectively. The coefficient of 1 in the diagonal is just a scaling parameter chosen so that utility is measured in terms of current dollars. For example, if, instead, utility from the point of view of $t = 2$ were expressed in terms of dollars at $t = 1$, the numbers in line 2 would be 0.5 and 0.25, the same numbers as in the corresponding columns of line 1. But this would make no difference for the individual's decisions, since what matters is how much one values a dollar in one period relative to another.

Proponents of hyperbolic discounting argue instead that the present is "salient" in that one is willing to forego fewer units of utility today in exchange for consumption tomorrow than when contemplating a trade-off between consumption tomorrow and consumption the day after tomorrow. Therefore, when next year arrives, I may decide that I prefer to consume the $100 after all rather than invest the money at 4 percent, although I would sincerely claim that I would be willing to invest them the following year. The incarnation of myself that is deciding to consume the $100 is in contradiction with the preceding one which promised to invest it instead.

Table 4.2. The Property of Hyperbolic Discounting

	$t = 1$	$t = 2$	$t = 3$
$t = 1$	1	0.4	0.2
$t = 2$		1	0.4
$t = 3$			1

Table 4.2 shows that if evaluated at $t = 1$, a dollar consumed at $t = 3$ is worth $0.2/0.4 = 0.5$ dollars consumed at $t = 2$. However, evaluated at $t = 2$, that dollar is now worth only 0.4 dollars of consumption at $t = 2$. The individual at $t = 2$ has different preferences from the individual at $t = 1$. The individual now has multiple selves. His incarnation at $t = 2$ disagrees with the $t = 1$ incarnation about the trade-off between consuming a dollar at $t = 2$ and a dollar at $t = 3$. Incarnation 2 is willing to sacrifice more units of consumption at $t = 3$ to increase consumption at $t = 2$ than Incarnation 1 is willing to sacrifice. In other words, Incarnation 1 would like Incarnation 2 to save more.

Proponents of hyperbolic discounting argue that it explains a range of phenomena such as the difficulty in getting rid of an addiction, procrastination, or holding an inconsistent portfolio where high-interest credit card debt coexists with low-yield assets. An important theme is that hyperbolic discounting will lead people to "undersave," which opens the door to government policies such as compulsory saving for retirement in the form of illiquid assets.

Mental Budgeting

Unitary individuals consider that "a dollar is a dollar"; they face a unique budget constraint which tells them that the sum of their expenses cannot exceed the sum of their revenues. Their behavior should not depend on the nature of their various income sources. An individual should have the same consumption behavior whether he earns $1,000 per month from his work and $1,000 per month from his financial investments, or $1,500 from his work and $500 from his financial investments.[4] Furthermore, whether the source of his financial wealth was winning a lottery or saving his hard-earned dollars should also be irrelevant. But researchers have found that people engage in mental budgeting, ascribing different income sources to different kinds of expenditure.[5] For example, they will use exceptional proceeds such as winning a lottery or having a higher wage bonus at the end of the year for "extra expenses" such as going to the restaurant, and their regular salary income will be used to pay for the rent and for clothes. Clearly that suggests a violation of rationality: if I have a wage cut of $100 per month but my bonus at the end of the year goes up by $1,200, my total income (neglecting interest) is unchanged. Yet if I engage in mental budgeting I am buying fewer clothes and going to the restaurant more often. With my well-defined preferences, this makes me more or less happy than before, depending on whether utility goes up or down. If it goes up, then I would have been better off spending my money on that new basket of goods when my wage was higher and my bonus lower, since I had the same income, so that purchasing that basket was feasible. Otherwise, I would be happier now by sticking to my previous consumption basket instead of buying fewer clothes and going to the restaurant more often. We again have a case of multiple selves: different incarnations are managing different needs. That phenomenon may help to explain paradoxes such as people feeling poorer even though statistics show that their total income has increased more than the relevant consumer price index. In principle, a consumer should always be better off in such a situation: by definition, he or she can always continue to buy the previous consumption basket, whose total price has risen less than the consumer's income, and such an action would make the individual just as well off. Since some money is left, it can be spent on additional items that make the individual strictly better off. But under mental budgeting, each self buys its own basket of goods, with its own price

[4] This is essentially the Modigliani-Miller theorem applied to the individual self. Note that it may also hold if there are multiple selves, provided those selves bargain between themselves (see chapter 12). In such a case they will pool their sources of income and treat them alike, and then redistribute consumption between themselves.

[5] See Heath and Soll 1996.

index. If the price of food, housing, and clothes increases by more than the corresponding income sources ascribed to these functions, then the self that cares about those needs can actually be worse off. If that self is "speaking" at the time a survey is being conducted, then the individual may report a fall in his living standards even though they have objectively gone up.

Intrinsic Motivation

Standard economics assumes that to motivate somebody to undertake costly actions (such as performing tasks on the job), he or she should be compensated by monetary rewards. By contrast, many psychologists and behavioral economists contend that motivation is often *intrinsic,* meaning that people derive rewards from the task itself, for example, the pleasure of accomplishment. Economists reply that if this were true, one would not need to be paid to work; although voluntary work exists, it is a minute part of economic activity. More important, intrinsic motivation does not a priori contradict the usual assumptions of economics. That people may derive pleasure from some aspects of their work simply means that they are willing to work longer or for a lower wage, or both, everything else being equal, than if it were not the case. As long as work is productive, firms are willing to offer a positive wage in exchange for it. Intrinsically motivated people will then supply extra hours beyond the level at which they are willing to work on the basis of their intrinsic motivation alone. In other words, I may happily work twenty hours for free but if the wage is $15 an hour I will increase my labor supply to forty hours. Hence intrinsic motivation and a positive monetary reward may coexist; this is not a paradox that invalidates the standard apparatus.

However, Frey and Benz (2001) highlight some aspects of intrinsic motivation that cannot be reconciled with the standard framework. The evidence they cite, and the experiments they run, suggest that monetary rewards *crowd out* intrinsic motivation—the *motivation transfer effect.* This takes place both across and within tasks. According to them, if I am offered monetary rewards I will no longer enjoy these twenty hours but instead consider that I am providing them in order to get the money as well. Furthermore, assuming that in addition to my work I was volunteering at some hospital, I will no longer be willing to volunteer in that hospital but will require compensation instead. My preferences, in other words, are no longer a given; they are shaped by my economic environment, including the price system and the contracts and reward structures I face.

Context Effects

A related theme is that preferences are determined by the context in which the choice has to be exerted. This is a radical departure from the assumption of "independence of irrelevant alternatives" defined in chapter 3. Like intrinsic motivation, context effects imply that preferences are no longer well defined independently of the institutional environment in which choices have to be made. There are two main themes here. First, preferences between two alternative choices may depend on the set of third alternatives that are available or on the way the choice problem is formulated or on both. Second, the well-being derived from an action (say, consuming a good) depends on how that action fares compared to some reference, that is, to what people expect. That reference is itself influenced by the person's past economic experiences, as well as his or her economic environment.[6]

For example, numerous empirical studies show that default options matter; that is, more generally, the *framing* of a decision problem—the way it is formulated—affects which decision is actually made, for a given set of alternatives. People who chose A over B if A is presented to them as the default option will often invert their choices and elect B if B is the default option. These findings have been used to advocate a number of policies, such as contributing to a pension fund being the default option in the relevant administrative forms or "healthy food" being presented more conspicuously in restaurants and cafeterias (a form of paternalism to which we return in part 2 of the book).

People are also thought to care about their relative economic status rather than their absolute one. That is, in fact, an old idea that goes back to at least Duesenberry's (1952) relative income hypothesis.[7] When that logic is applied across time, it means that people use their past economic achievements (say, income level) to evaluate their current ones, a mechanism we will refer to, borrowing from Layard (2003), as *habituation.* Being richer yesterday raises my "expectations" today, which tends to make me less happy. Having $10,000 makes me less happy today if I had $20,000 yesterday than having $9,000 if I had $8,000 yesterday. This property is referred to as *loss aversion.* Clearly traditional economic theory would instead predict that $9,000 is worth less than $10,000. Loss aversion occurs because the reference level that defines what people expect is often defined by the status quo. Thaler (1980) and Kahneman, Knetsch, and Thaler (1990) have shown, for example, that people value a good more immediately after they have acquired it. This is called the *endowment effect.* Kahneman and his coauthors randomly distributed mugs that were worth $5 to students—not all students got one. They then managed to find the price at which those who had a mug where willing to sell it, and the price at which those who did not have a mug wanted to buy it. Because the mugs were randomly distributed, one would expect that those who had a mug did not like it more than those who did not have one. In other words, we expect the selling price to be the same, on average, as the buying price and not too different from the

---

[6] The idea that people value outcomes relative to some reference level can be formulated in a variety of contexts and is referred to as using a variety of labels. One version is "prospect theory," proposed by Kahneman and Tversky (1979).

[7] This idea is also present in Keynes's General Theory as a justification of nominal wage rigidity.

market price of $5. But the authors found that the sellers asked for $7 on average, and buyers offered $3.50. These results suggest that the status quo of having a mug defines a reference point for the sellers, which increases the value they place on it.

If we now apply that logic across individuals, it implies that the greater the consumption level of others, the less happy people are, which we shall call *rivalry*. Experimental evidence and studies of self-reported happiness indeed show that such phenomena exist.

Researchers have found that measured levels of happiness do not go up with conventional measures of well-being such as consumption and income. Brickman, Coates, and Janoff-Bulman (1978), for example, find no difference between the self-reported happiness levels of lottery winners and a control group of nonwinners. One standard interpretation of those findings is that winning the lottery increases the reference consumption level that winners expect, and it is the difference between actual consumption and that reference level that determines happiness.

Context effects do not mean, a priori, that people are irrational. They can sometimes be reconciled with a bona fide utility function, in the same fashion as addiction. For example, the idea that my past consumption serves as a reference level for my current one can be embodied in a utility function for today which decreases with my past consumption level. Rational consumers will then recognize such effects and weigh the present gains of consuming more today versus the future losses from having a higher reference level (in addition to the usual future losses coming from the reduction in savings). This is very similar to the argument on rational addiction discussed in chapter 3, and there is, in fact, a large literature in standard economics that studies the consequences of such "habit formation."[8] In most of the debate about such context effects, however, people are considered not to be aware of them—and that is often on empirical grounds. A consumer unaware of his own habit formation will then behave as if consisting of multiple selves, since his current self will maximize an incorrect utility function, failing to internalize the fact that in the future he will be prone to habit formation.

Confidence-Enhanced Performance

It has also been documented that context effects not only have an impact on individual welfare but also on individual competence. It is known, for example, that the fear of failure negatively affects performance. A general view among psychologists is that self-esteem and overconfidence promote achievement. For a unitary individual, productivity is considered to be independent of beliefs. If I think I will fail at an enterprise I will not want to undertake it, but that is

---

[8] An example is Abel 1990.

because I have computed that the costs of this project outweigh its benefits, not because my beliefs affect my talent at performing the required tasks associated with it. Instead, psychologists have found that people who think they might fail show signs of stress that reduce their brain's capacity to process signals and therefore hamper their actions. In other words, considering the possibility of failing affects people's mood in such a way that they are less good at performing tasks.

Compte and Postlewaite (2004) study an analytical model where they show that if confidence enhances performance, then individuals with a cognitive bias toward optimism will perform better than nonbiased individuals. Since we know that many people are cognitively dissonant and tend to rationalize past decisions and be overconfident, these findings may shed some light as to why biased individuals have evolved: their disadvantage in terms of making informed rational decisions is offset by the advantages conferred by confidence in terms of achievements. This model does not tell us, however, why these types have evolved rather than types who are *both* confident and with no cognitive biases; perhaps it is cheaper—that is, requires less work in terms of mutation—for Nature to hardwire a link between confidence and performance rather than evolving large computational capabilities that will lead people to make the right decisions if given the right information. For my purpose, the most notable aspect of that phenomenon is that people subject to these biases have a rational interest in *fooling* themselves that they have greater chances of succeeding than in reality. That is presumably why some politicians don't look at polls during an election campaign, or some actors do not read the critics as long as a play is on stage. But fooling oneself is nevertheless a difficult task.

The behavioral aspects most relevant to my argument in this book are those that are not reducible to a unitary utility function that would be modified to embody these exotic phenomena. In such cases, the revealed preferences principle—the tight link between actions and preferences—no longer holds. It is no longer possible to claim that if an individual chooses a course of action, it is preferable for him to any other alternative available. At best, one of his "incarnations" made the decision, regardless of the (potentially adverse) effects of that choice on the individual's other incarnations. At worst, the individual is driven by neurological processes and one could even argue that his choices are objectively harming him.

An important consequence is that the presumption in favor of laissez-faire epitomized in the First and Second Welfare Theorems is no longer granted. That failure is pervasive across a spectrum of economic issues.

It is quite possible to consider behavioral economics as a purely positive science that describes individual behavior without drawing any policy consequence. However, it will often be used to analyze and advocate policies, which brings about two important issues: How do we define individual welfare in a behavioral world? And how do we define the preferences of "society"?

5

From Utility to Happiness

From the observation that, because revealed preferences fail, actions cannot be used as the basis of a theory of individual welfare, it is natural to propose, as an alternative, that one should use some direct measure of individual well-being, such as happiness. The recent literature on behavioral economics includes a growing research on its determinants. In general, proponents of this approach claim that they are measuring the relevant utility, that is, the flow of an individual's well-being, in a direct way. Some authors see a superiority over revealed preferences even independently of the psychological phenomena discussed in the preceding chapter, in that revealed preferences measure well-being only if the assumption of a rational utility-maximizing individual is correct, whereas measures of happiness would, by definition, directly measure utility. To quote Easterlin (2003):

> A basic problem with the revealed preference approach is that the judgment on a person's well-being is made, not by the individual concerned, but by an outsider who is observing the person's consumption choices. [...] If one takes the view that the only one who can make authoritative observations on a person's feelings of well-being is the person concerned, then one is led to look at self reports on well-being.

This critique misses the point of revealed preferences, which is to allow us to make statements about the utility from a decision that has been made over a decision that has *not* been made. Direct measures of happiness tell us nothing about how happy people would feel if instead they were earning less, consuming a different basket of goods, or not be married to the same person. At best, they allow us to compare self-reported happiness between today and last year, but since moving backward in time is not an option, that does not allow us to infer that there is any self-harm in the course of action taken by the individual.

Measures of self-reported happiness can be problematic. The answers can reflect what people think they are supposed to say, rather than their true feelings. These expectations can vary across people, cultures, and economic circumstances. This can generate all sorts of biases. For example, a rich person can state that he or she is happy just because the culture considers that being richer makes you happier; or the person could report the contrary, out of fear of envy or because of some preconceived ideas against wealth inherited from the person's culture.

Notably, however, one is able to measure happiness directly by observing brain activity. Davidson, Jackson, and Kalin (2000) have used electro-encephalographic evidence to show that "positive feelings correspond to brain activity in the left side of the prefrontal cortex, somewhat above and in front of the ear. And negative feelings correspond to brain activity in the same place on the right side of the brain." (Layard 2003). Subjects have been shown pleasant pictures (a baby smiling) and unpleasant pictures (a baby with a face damaged by an accident). The nice pictures stimulate brain activity in the left side, and the ugly ones stimulate the right side. The issue is clearly far from settled. Such an experiment is quite different from asking people whether they are satisfied with their life or how they feel. But my point here is not to engage in methodological issues and argue that this evidence is unreliable; it may well be that it is indeed misleading and that the unitary model of the individual can be saved after all. Instead, I want to highlight the dangers of relying on measured happiness as a central pillar of social welfare, even if it were correctly measured. So let us assume that self-reported happiness is truthful. What do these studies find?

Many of the findings emphasize the importance of context effects and other mechanisms that deviate from the individual's standard rational view; together with the rejection of revealed preferences, this opens the door for recommendations of paternalistic interventions that supposedly increase welfare.

Let us go back to the relative income hypothesis, which focuses on an intrapersonal context effect: the effect of past consumption or income on current consumption aspirations. In the extreme, if the reference consumption level of an individual increases dollar-for-dollar with his income, then his happiness, which is related to the difference between the actual consumption level and the reference one, cannot go up with income.

Empirically many studies corroborate the view that "money does not buy happiness." Easterlin (2003) reports that, over their life cycle, richer people report higher average happiness than poorer people; however, within the life cycle, self-reported happiness is flat: people do not report a higher satisfaction level as they get richer. He then connects those findings with evidence that as people get richer, new aspirations (such as a bigger car, a second mobile phone, a flat TV) appear. Are these new aspirations strong enough to push us to the extreme case where "money does not buy happiness"? According to Rainwater (1994), the answer should be yes. He compares reported "get along" income with actual income and finds an elasticity of one: which means that aspirations, expressed in monetary terms, go up one for one with actual income.

In contrast, aspirations appear to be less elastic to outcomes when one deals with nonpecuniary goals such as health or marital fulfillment. Thus a divorce or serious disease permanently reduces reported happiness, whereas a permanent reduction in income should, according to these authors, only have transitory effects.

From there one is tempted to conclude that the whole concern of modern households with material well-being and the policy maker's obsession with the gross domestic product (GDP), employment, and growth are pointless and that Western economies should mimic Bhutan or even revert to the Stone Age. Indeed, Easterlin and others are quick to conclude that people allocate their time inadequately between economic pursuits, where the associated increase in aspirations quickly dissipates any gain in happiness, and other "higher" goals such as being in good health, having a fulfilling family life, or enjoying the arts: "With regard to macroeconomic policy, reducing unemployment and inflation increases happiness, but the pursuit of rapid economic growth as a policy objective is questionable" [...] "As a result, most individuals spend a disproportionate amount of time working, and sacrifice family life and health, domains in which aspirations remain fairly constant as actual circumstances change, and where the attainment of one's goals has a more lasting effect on happiness" (Easterlin 2003). It is all too natural, then, that a government, on the basis of the recommendations of those who have researched what makes people happy, imposes taxes on activities that reduce happiness and subsidizes activities that increase it.

How can we reconcile the evidence that richer people are happier than poorer people with the evidence that a single individual is not made happier, except transitorily, by income gains? The answer, according to proponents of happiness research, is that this is the result of both habituation and rivalry (See Layard 2003). When others consume more relative to me, I feel less happy. When I consume more relative to others, I feel happier. Thus relatively richer people are happier, but making everybody richer by the same proportion would make nobody happier, because aspirations would grow up proportionally, both because people will get used to their own higher consumption level and because they will see their rivals enjoy a similar rise in consumption.

A number of studies document rivalry effects in self-reported happiness. Solnick and Hemenway (1998) have asked graduate students whether they would be happier with $50,000 a year if others only get half that money versus $100,000 a year if others make twice that amount. The majority preferred the first option. The answers contradict the standard model: with $100,000 a year I can buy the same basket of goods as with $50,000, plus some other things. Therefore my utility should necessarily go up. Blanchflower and Oswald (2000) find similar effects by comparing U.S. states: they find that the average income in the state where you live has a significant negative impact on your self-reported happiness.

As in the case of habituation, the evidence suggests that relative comparisons are less important for nonpecuniary dimensions of welfare. Thus Solnick and Hemenway ask the graduate students another question, namely, whether they would prefer two weeks of vacation, provided others have half that time, versus four weeks, provided others have twice that amount of time. They find that only 20 percent of participants would choose the first option.

It is also true that absolute income starts mattering if one falls below a certain income level. This is presumably because fundamental needs such as health, food, and clothes are an important determinant of happiness at low income levels. Hence Inglehart and Klingemann (2000) report a very strong effect of a country's GDP on its average reported happiness for income levels below $10,000 in the 1990s. The relationship becomes much flatter, although still arguably positive, past that threshold.[1]

It is also possible to widen the scope of happiness studies by using large individual databases of self-reported happiness and compute, using econometric techniques, the effect on happiness of a number of variables capturing both the individual's personal situation and his environment. Helliwell (2001) has used a large database of individuals in different countries to estimate the impact of those variables. His work can be used to compute the estimated impact on happiness of a number of factors. Table 5.1, borrowed from Layard (2003), tells us how many "points" of happiness one gains (or loses) from a change in one's situation.[2] Here, one "point" of happiness is defined as the gain from experiencing a 50 percent income gain (or, equivalently, the loss from a 33 percent income loss).[3]

Table 5.1. Various Determinants of Happiness

Before	After	Change in Happiness
Employed	Unemployed	−3
Secure job	Insecure job	−1.5
Married	Divorced	−2.5
5% unemployment rate	15% unemployment rate	−1.5
5% inflation rate	15% inflation rate	−0.5
Dictature (Belarus)	Democracy (Hungary)	+2.5

Source: Layard 2003.

These results can be compared to Easterlin's conclusion that there are "fundamental" aspects of life that matter more than income, and that the emphasis on economic achievements and the GDP is misplaced. In fact, the results seem

---

[1] Layard (2003) focuses on the countries with a yearly income per head greater than $15,000 and argues that, for these countries, there is no relationship at all. True, but they are quite similar and all we can say is that, for this subsample, a statistical test that income does not matter for one to be happy is not rejected. But the hypothesis that income has a positive effect on happiness over the whole $10,000 to $30,000 range is not rejected either, even though the slope is smaller than for countries with a yearly income per head below $10,000. In other words, one cannot reject that this is a stable relationship that also holds for the subsample of richer countries.

[2] The original studies on which these numbers are based are Helliwell 2001; and Blanchflower and Oswald 2000. The effects of the variables considered are partially controlling for income. Thus the effect on happiness of being unemployed reflects the contribution of unemployment per se and not that of the consequences of unemployment on income.

[3] The equivalent loss may, in fact, be lower if there is loss aversion.

almost too good to be believed. The first row suggests that people would feel exactly as happy earning $10,000 a year while employed as they would if they were unemployed but earned $25,000. The second row indicates that workers are willing to have a 50 percent pay cut in exchange for job security. And that is also how much they would pay to bring the unemployment rate down by 10 points, even though unions in continental Europe have typically opposed much smaller wage cuts that would have helped create jobs. Finally, people seem willing to pay a lot for political freedom; they are willing to sacrifice more than half their income to be in a democracy rather than a dictatorship. Yet it is unclear just how relevant formal political freedoms remain for an average person who has lost half of his or her purchasing power.

▌ Interpreting Happiness Studies

Numerous interpretation problems stem from the fact that the outcome of the mind's rational activity and emotions are not insulated from each other. For example, the students in the above-mentioned study by Solnick and Hemenway may have simply worked out the economic consequences of others being twice as rich as they are: higher housing prices, medical costs, and so on. They may well have concluded that even with a conventional, context-independent utility, they would be worse off, after all, with $100,000 if others were twice as rich than with $50,000 if others were twice as poor. And many of the "nonpecuniary" things (leisure, health, and even marital stability) that supposedly bring real rather than spurious happiness can largely be bought with money.

Or people may be rational and report "happiness" not as how they feel but as a judgement about how well they are doing relative to a reference point that represents how well they *could* do. "Aspirations" are no longer interpreted as a phenomenon of envy or habituation but as the *information* people have about their feasible set of outcomes. If I get a big pay rise, I infer that I am more productive than I thought, and I now expect to make more. If I then am reduced to my previous pay, it means I am performing below my potential—in other words, I am not optimizing correctly, and that is clearly annoying and frustrating. If I had not gotten the increase in pay, I would have no reason to believe that I am making mistakes in my optimization. Similarly, if that friend with whom I went to college just bought a big car I cannot afford, it means he undertook actions that were available to me and that I failed to see. His status reveals the mistakes I made in conducting my life. Clearly the more he and I are in "the same league," the greater the informational content in my neighbor's success. If my neighbor had been a prodigy at school, I would not have minded that he became a millionaire at age twenty. This is because his expected success reveals nothing about whether I have made the right decisions. If such a hypothesis is correct, then people in happiness surveys are reporting their perceived performance in optimizing their choices. There is indeed empirical evidence that rivalry effects are stronger between people of similar backgrounds. As Layard puts it: "What matters is what happens to your 'reference group' because what your reference group gets might have been feasible for you." This is perfectly consistent with the rational interpretation we just discussed.[4]

It is even possible that such a judgment is hardwired, meaning that my neighbor's success will make me feel bad in a measurable, chemical sense. The happiness studies would then be perfectly accurate. The bad feelings are a cue I get from my environment, which may lead me to act in order to improve my situation—that is, get closer to the optimal outcome I can hope for given my skills and constraints. One can spell out a simple evolutionary argument explaining such hardwiring: Those who did not feel bad when witnessing success by similar individuals did not react adequately and achieved a lower fitness level. Consequently, they passed their genes with less success than those who experience feelings of rivalry.

Consider the following example: Mary lives in a dangerous neighborhood. As a result of that, she experiences depression and stress. Her happiness level is low. She comes to see a psychiatrist, who ignores the fact that her depression has an objective cause. The psychiatrist is sincerely interested in raising her feeling of well-being. So he might envisage some psychotherapy or even medicate her with Prozac. Mary now feels much better. According to happiness economics, her utility flow has measurably increased. She ticks a more upbeat box in surveys, and there are more flashes in her left brain. The psychiatrist has implemented "good" policy. But one day Mary is brutally assaulted by a gang of thugs and ends up with irreparable damage. The medication has suppressed her emotional warnings about her environment being objectively unsafe. Feeling well thanks to Prozac, she did not take any steps to move to a safer neighborhood.

▎ The Happiness = Utility Fallacy

This example illustrates the fundamental point that, contrary to what most happiness researchers claim, utility is different from happiness.[5] Utility is a useful abstract concept that summarizes our goals, and therefore what we *want*. Hap-

---

[4] It is interesting to compare this discussion to Nozick's views on envy and self-esteem. He also recognizes that self-esteem results from comparing oneself to a relevant reference group, although he does not interpret low self-esteem as recognition of the failure to implement the most efficient actions. He also holds that human nature is such that people will always pick some dimension along which to compare themselves with others. Thus any attempt to eliminate envy by equalizing outcomes in some dimension (as proponents of happiness research often advocate) will be defeated, as people will compare themselves along some other dimension. See Nozick 1974, chap. 8. Note that happiness researchers would dispute that claim, since they believe that for some dimensions (health, marriage, etc.) people care about their absolute status and not their relative one.

[5] Of course, one may always redefine happiness as utility. But then it becomes a tautology; interpreting self-reported happiness as utility is an article of faith; and one can no longer interpret neurological evidence as measuring utility, unless one assumes that people indeed maximize the flow of positive feelings as measured by those techniques.

piness is just a mental state: how we *feel*. People surely prefer to feel well than not to feel well, but not at any cost. Feeling well is one of their goals, but they have other goals as well. Status, ambition, survival, wealth accumulation, building a family, testing one's physical and intellectual limits, and achieving fame are other goals that are equally respectable, and often more respectable, than just feeling well. Only the individual can make a statement about the relative importance of those goals. In identifying utility with happiness, researchers are making their own paternalistic statement that individuals should care more about feeling well, relative to other goals, than they actually do.

The happiness literature finds that it is the shift in aspirations that makes people unhappy as their past consumption or their neighbor's consumption goes up, and concludes that this is a form of pollution that should be prevented. If one takes this seriously, aspirations should be set as low as possible. The homeless are then quite happy, since they presumably do not long for a big house and a big car. Therefore global happiness would go up if we had more street people. Instead, one may more plausibly consider that aspirations, just like feelings, enter the utility function in that they affect what people want. People routinely put themselves in situations where they know they will experience bad feelings, when they seek to break a record, win a football match, get a job, or get promoted. And what about the masochists?

A happiness researcher would probably object to my argument that when experiencing pain out of their own decisions, people are actually investing in future rewards. Perhaps the masochist feels an overwhelming flow of happiness when being released from pain. The happiness researcher would then go on to argue that because of people's cognitive biases they overestimate those future happiness flows, as the evidence on happiness over the life cycle or on lottery winners shows.[6] However, this is just one specific interpretation of the findings: if people are not made happier from having bought that big house, and if acquiring it was painful, it must be that they have made a mistake. But another interpretation may just be that they knew perfectly well that it would not make them happier, but they decided to go for status rather than feelings. Therefore they did not make a mistake; they just care less about their own happiness than the expert who is studying their behavior. We could spell out a list of reasons why they would rationally prefer the bigger house even though it does not trigger flashes in their left brain. Perhaps their children would be safer and more comfortable, or perhaps they would make a better career out of the connections they would establish in that wealthier neighborhood.

---

[6] Here the reader may note that different prescriptions from different brands of behavioral economics need not agree. Although happiness research sometimes suggests that people overinvest because they fail to recognize that the future returns from their investment are plagued by habituation, the typical conclusion of approaches based on hyperbolic discounting is that they are more likely to underinvest, since they put too much weight on current rewards rather than deferred ones. Hyperbolic discounting and happiness research agree that John should not get this new flashy car, but they disagree about John's attempt to get an MBA.

The evolutionary interpretation of happiness further highlights the short-comings in seeking to maximize it as a foundation for government policy. From the perspective of evolutionary psychology, a feeling of happiness should be "adaptive," that is, "good." We have already seen, as Mary's example above suggests, that negative feelings are also "adaptive," implying that suppressing them artificially may objectively be harmful to the individual. Two additional considerations are likely to introduce discrepancies between happiness and the individual's objective interest.

First of all, the environment evolves more quickly than genes so that positive feelings that used to hardwire an adaptive response in the past may now be counterproductive. One may think of aggressive impulses, or propensities to accumulate sugar or fat. It is then in the individual's interest to reduce their perceived happiness in order to enhance their objective survival rate in the long run.

Second, evolutionary psychology states that people's behavior is driven by their need to pass their genes. Thus behaviors evolve that maximize the individual's *inclusive fitness*, the fraction of his or her genes that are passed to the subsequent generation. The concept of inclusive fitness is tricky: I am driven not to pass the actual physical genes that are in my DNA (this is materially impossible) but any *copy* of them. Thus individuals are not selfish; only their genes are selfish[7]. A selfish individual will not risk a 50 percent chance of dying to save the life of his identical twin brother. But an individual maximizing inclusive fitness would do that if that increased the twin's survival chance from 20 percent to 90 percent. That is because the identical twin has the same DNA as the individual, and what is maximized is the fraction of that piece of information that is passed to the next generation.

Because inclusive rather than individual fitness is being maximized, I may be hardwired to undertake actions that objectively harm me as an individual, even though those actions benefit my "selfish genes" through the enhanced survival rates of my "kin" (siblings, children, etc.). And those actions may be triggered by positive feelings. This is presumably the reason why we observe phenomena such as sacrifice, religious fanatics and suicide bombers, although the instincts that drive them probably no longer maximize their own inclusive fitness as they once did in the past, when the environment was harsher and human groups were smaller and more genetically connected. In any case, it would be problematic for society to value these actions just because they are associated with positive feelings. If a technology for turning these feelings off existed, many individuals would want to use it even though it might reduce the flow of positive feelings experienced over their lifetime.[8]

---

[7] The most popular reference here is evidently Dawkins 1976.

[8] This conclusion is uncontroversial if the feeling no longer enhances inclusive fitness because the environment is now different, regardless of whether it acts through the individual's own survival prospects versus some altruistic sacrifice in favor of his kin. But the issue becomes far trickier if we were in a situation where the feelings trigger an altruistic response that harms the individual while still benefiting his selfish genes. Should the individual emancipate himself from the selfish

Conversely, bad feelings lead us to want less of the same so that we take actions that may change a situation that is harmful for our fitness. That is what Mary is doing if she moves out of her neighborhood. In some sense, it is totally consistent with the view that Mary is pursuing happiness. Moving out of the neighborhood is an investment into future higher happiness. But the point is that the bad feeling should not be considered a bad thing *as such*. As a self-help website[9] puts it, "Research suggests that stress can actually increase our performance. Instead of wilting under stress, one can use it as an impetus to achieve success. Stress can stimulate one's faculties to delve deep into and discover one's true potential. Under stress the brain is emotionally and biochemically stimulated to sharpen its performance."

Thus both positive and negative feelings are signals meant to trigger an adaptive reaction. One may want to suppress some of them, even though they are positive, because they are no longer relevant to inclusive fitness in the contemporary environment. And one may not want to suppress some others, even though they are negative, because they still play a useful role. Maximizing the positive feelings and minimizing the negative feelings incorrectly considers feelings as a goal in itself rather than signals aimed at triggering an appropriate response.

Arguably economics was "archaic" prior to the behavioral developments discussed in chapters 4 and 5. Rather than a science, it was a philosophical system grounded on mathematics or at least logics, which (among other things) provided foundations for limited government. Its attempt to be scientific, however, made it vulnerable to confrontation with the data and susceptible to evolution. The recent evolution makes economics look more like a modern science than an eighteenth-century–style philosophical system. But it also shows how weak its utilitarian basis for limited government is. And once this basis is eliminated on empirical grounds, economics joins other social sciences in paving the way for paternalism.

gene and "rationally" invest in a technology that turns off those altruistic instincts? Or should he stick to "gene rationality" and accept sacrifice, which in addition to higher inclusive fitness yields positive rewards in terms of feelings? In my view, we do not have to take a stand on this. People are free to pursue happiness, survival of their organism, inclusive fitness, or other goals. The key point is that there is no ground for putting happiness first by means of "training" and other government interventions.

9 http://www.lifepositive.com/stress.html (accessed November 17, 2010).

Part II

The Rise of Paternalism

The development of behavioral economics and happiness research undermines the "last bastion" of rationality. This is likely to lead to a new approach to social welfare and a new set of policy prescriptions. The following chapters analyze the logic of this new approach and its connection with the rise of paternalism and the curtailment of individual freedom. I highlight how the paternalistic policies are guided by utilitarian principles that are modified in order to take into account the pervasive view that individuals are not unitary and suffer from behavioral bias. I consider how behavioral economics, in particular, contributes to this trend and provides justifications for the paternalistic policies. Thus the overall picture is that of a consistent mutual interaction between the development of social sciences, society's general conceptions about human nature, and the increasing intrusiveness of government. That said, one should avoid making too much of explanatory systems. While this mechanism surely accounts for a substantial share of what we observe, other forces are at work. At one extreme of the spectrum, some policy makers just impose undesired outcomes on people because of their own preconceived ideas of what is "good," without reference to any intellectual framework. At the other extreme, some social scientists are studying behavioral biases without advocating paternalism or even while being frankly opposed to it.

What is paternalism? Clearly we cannot reduce this to the notion that some individuals disagree with the policies that are undertaken; that would make paternalism a notion identical to the lack of a Pareto improvement, which would be useless. For example, income redistribution harms some individuals and benefits others, and yet its motivations are seldom paternalistic. Therefore we need to be more explicit about what we mean by paternalism.

One natural definition of paternalism—let us call it strong paternalism—is that it constrains behavior beyond its sheer effect on people's budget constraints and the prices they face. In other words, one can conceive of a rational individual who would change his or her behavior if the policy we consider were removed, while having the same income and facing the same prices.[1] Thus redistribution of income, or Pigovian taxation to correct an externality, are not strongly paternalistic. In both cases people freely dispose of their income and are in the same situation if, absent the policy, they face the same net income and prices as under the policy. Thus by revealed preference, they will make the same choices. Note, however, the important proviso that we only consider rational

[1] This is a thought experiment that ignores the fact that if the policy were removed, all prices would change and therefore nobody would have the same income and prices as before. The thought experiment asks how a single rational individual would change his or her behavior should one be able to remove the policy while leaving the prices faced by that individual unchanged; in other words, it ignores the adjustment of the economic equilibrium that would happen should one indeed remove the policy. In the case of a tax on smoking, if it were removed the price of cigarettes would presumably fall, so that even a rational individual would smoke more. All that the criterion is saying in such a case is that were the tax removed but the price unchanged for some reason, these individuals would not change their behavior.

individuals. Irrational individuals may well change their mind because of context effects, if we replace the policy by a situation that is equivalent in terms of income and prices. Thus if we were applying that definition to irrational individuals, virtually any policy would be paternalistic. Here, forcing everybody to wear a yellow tie is strongly paternalistic: people who hate yellow ties will not wear them if left free to choose. But a tax on smoking, even though it may be motivated by paternalistic concerns, will not be strongly paternalistic. Rational individuals only care about prices, and if those are unchanged they will not change their choices. The tax deters them from smoking because the price of cigarettes is high, which is all they care about. They would not smoke more if the price were equally high for some reason other than taxes.

Clearly any intervention that makes use of taxes and transfers, rather than regulatory constraints, cannot be paternalistic according to that definition. Yet many of the policies that are advocated by paternalists have such a form, and they would not advocate those taxes if they thought that people behave responsibly. Hence it may be useful to think about how such policies—those that use the tax system to correct for behavioral biases—differ from those that use the same instruments to redistribute income or correct for objective market failures. This leads me to the definition of *weak paternalism.* We want our definition to reflect the fact that a paternalistic policy would be inefficient, if only the irrational people could overcome their behavioral problems. This suggests that an appropriate definition would be close to that of a lack of Pareto optimality: that is, if some external hand could force the irrational agents to do what is "best" for them, then one could make everybody better off by removing the policy. In other words, the policy only works because of the agents that are subject to biases. For example, the tax on smoking could be too high, from the perspective of rational smokers, because too many of them decide not to smoke, which reduces their utility. But the high tax deters compulsive smokers from entering a consumption path hazardous for their wealth. If those compulsive smokers could overcome their psychological issues on their own, they would reduce their cigarette consumption even at lower tax levels. Reducing the tax would then be Pareto improving relative to the initial situation where the tax is very high and compulsive smokers cannot commit: the rational smokers will be able to smoke more (which *increases* their welfare, despite the fact that such a statement may seem strange in the current context).[2] The others are, by assumption, compelled to do what is best for them, so their welfare has to increase. The problem, though, is that the irrational individuals do not generally have a well-defined utility function. Therefore we cannot use the fact that their

[2] In this example, I neglect the role of tax revenues. A lower tax on cigarettes will lower tax revenues, unless the tax is so high that it is on the wrong side of the Laffer curve. In any case, for the tax to be paternalistic, it must be higher than the one that would be optimal absent the behavioral biases. This means that if these biases are solved by some other devices, it must be optimal to reduce the tax; in some cases this may entail compensating for the loss of revenues by raising some other tax that is less distortionary.

If behavioral biases are fixed, & there exist an optimal tax X, any tax > X is paternalistic

welfare may improve in our definition. We can observe, however, that revealed preferences would apply to them, should they be rational. Therefore, if their preceding outcomes are still available in their new choice set, they are better off should they maximize any unitary utility function. In that sense, we know that removing the paternalistic policy while leaving their previous choices available cannot make them worse off if they learn how to "behave," at least when this is evaluated using the unitary utility function that describes their choices under such self-discipline.

Therefore we will say that a policy is weakly paternalistic if an alternative policy exists such that the outcome under the paternalistic policy is feasible for all nonrational agents; and all rational agents are at least as well off, and one of them at least is strictly better off.

Note that if there are no irrational agents in society, this definition boils down to the non-Pareto optimality of the initial allocation of resources. Also, both definitions become void if there are no rational agents in society.

The following chapters discuss the logic and the evolution of the modern paternalistic state. I first consider how the notion of social welfare is likely to be redefined, and the implications in terms of policy prescriptions. I then depict, on the basis of current real-world developments, how the new society is being organized, particularly with respect to the role of the welfare state, the evolution of individual responsibility, the use of science, and the regulation of markets.

In a nutshell, the paternalistic society rests on four basic tenets that all derive from the premise that individuals are not unitary:

- People need the intervention of a third party to solve their behavioral issues. The state is a natural third party.
- Experts can study the actual effects of actions on individual welfare and make a better choice on behalf of the individual.
- Any ex-post incentive scheme based on making people liable for the consequences of their past actions will fail. Instead, we need ex-ante schemes that immediately tax and reward people for the future (potential) consequences of their current actions that they are not able to internalize.
- How people feel is more relevant for policy than what they want and what they do.

In my opinion, with these four ingredients in hand, we have a good recipe for tyranny.

Post-Utilitarianism: Searching for a Collective Soul in the Behavioral Era

If, as behavioral economics and other social sciences contend, we cannot trust people to make responsible choices according to their own well-defined preferences, how can any policy advice be implemented? People who want to formulate advice need to reconstruct some notion of collective preferences. To date, there is no equivalent of the fundamental welfare theorems that would provide a scientific basis for defining the scope of government intervention, if one no longer assumes the validity of revealed preferences. Therefore, as we shall see, the policy prescriptions that stem from behavioral economics are piecemeal rather than principled. However, they obey at least some underlying logic, which it is important to discuss. Inevitably some more explicit principles will arise so as to guide government intervention, which will be the result of the interactions between actual policies and academic debates. We want to have an idea of what these new foundations will look like, for this will have consequences for how much individual freedom will be left.

In what follows I highlight four main possibilities. Each of those possibilities is a potential solution to the problem of defining an objective for public policy in a world without well-defined preferences. Even though those approaches differ, it will be useful in the rest of the book to contrast them with traditional utilitarianism by grouping them under a single heading. I will therefore refer to this as the *post-utilitarian* paradigm, defined as the attempt to reconstruct social preferences when individuals have behavioral issues.[1]

These four possibilities are as follows:

- First, one may want to reinterpret behavioral biases so as to make them compatible with the standard framework by interpreting them as rational phenomena (as in the case of rational addiction) or as a subjective form

[1] Now it is quite possible to advocate policies without any reference to some concept of collective welfare; for example, arguably, in Marxist approaches a peculiar form of social organization is a goal in itself, and that organization is not derived from a collective notion of well-being. But if one remains in the tradition of the economics and political science of the Enlightenment, one cannot escape the challenge of providing foundations for social preferences.

of an externality. In this case, the standard apparatus and its associated welfare theorems, as described in chapter 3, are unchanged. The only novelty is that one applies it to objects that are a bit more exotic than initially thought.

- A second approach considers each individual as made up of multiple selves and then simply aggregates the utility of all incarnations in society, in the same way as a utilitarian social planner would aggregate the utility of all individuals.
- A third possibility is to give up on aggregating utility and consider as legitimate only policies that improve the welfare of all incarnations, that is, Pareto-improving policies.
- Finally, a fourth possibility is to redefine the social welfare function as the total flow of happiness in society, irrespective of any notion of individual choice.

A. Revamping a Utility-Based Social Welfare Function

When facing individual behavioral issues, one can try to keep using a utilitarian social welfare function but modify it by either making use of a less conventional—but nevertheless unique—utility function or treating behavioral issues as externalities.

Let us, for example, go back to the relative income hypothesis. We shall start with the habituation effect. If people are aware of it, they will recognize that greater consumption today makes them less happy in the future because their aspirations will grow, and that will prompt them to moderate consumption. We are then back to our discussion of rational addiction, where people are now addicted to consumption in general rather than consumption of a particular good. As we have seen, this does not violate standard economic results;[2] therefore the first and second welfare theorems continue to hold, and there is no further scope for paternalistic government intervention than is predicted by conventional economic theory.

How about rivalry? Rivalry can be introduced in a conventional social welfare function by assuming that the welfare of an individual depends on other people's income or consumption levels. This is somewhat unconventional because preferences should in principle be context-free. Formally, however, the mechanism works exactly like a standard externality such as environmental pollution. Consider two economies; let us call them "Oceania" and "Eurasia."

---

[2] One may naturally be tempted to confuse habituation with behavioral biases. The reason is that the existence of, say, hyperbolic discounting is likely to magnify the costs of habituation, since a hyperbolic discounter will not pay proper attention to habituation. Hyperbolic discounting, however, creates inefficiencies even absent habituation—confer the undersaving problem—and habituation does not invalidate any of the welfare theorems if people are unitary and rational. Thus the two issues are clearly different.

In Oceania, the average income in society reduces my utility because my flow of happiness depends on my relative status. In Eurasia, the average income in society reduces my utility because producing goods involves environmental degradation. Whereas the economy of Eurasia is plagued by a traditional externality, in Oceania people have nonstandard preferences as their psychological mood depends on the context. Yet these two economies could be represented by the same (in mathematical terms) economic model, and, for a given social welfare function, a similar tax would correct pollution in Eurasia and envy in Oceania.

This example illustrates how conspicuous consumption can be treated as just another form of pollution because it makes other people "feel bad."[3]

This solution is bound to be imperfect, for two reasons. First, there is an operational issue in basing policies on subjective considerations. Traditionally economic theory considered that utility only depended on objective outcomes, such as consumption, leisure, and so on. Similarly the externalities that were considered were also objective, such as pollution, noise, or productive externalities. Since, ultimately, the goods are valued by a subjective self, there is no a priori reason why one should exclude subjective goods, such as feelings, from the utility function,[4] and this validates treating psychological phenomena, such as rivalry, as externalities. However, it will be far more difficult for policy makers to *price* this kind of externality in order to put in place corrective taxes than with objective externalities. One could only rely on self-reported damages, but these would easily be manipulated by the "victims" of the externality in order to enhance their compensation. Second, some psychological biases are not reducible to a psychological externality or a refinement of a standard utility function; therefore the approach only addresses a subset of the issues raised by behavioral sciences.

▌ B. Aggregating between Incarnations

The solution of keeping a standard social welfare function, augmented for new kinds of externalities and sophisticated formulations aimed at capturing psychological phenomena in a rational way, no longer holds if individuals indeed

---

[3] The difference between introducing subjective externalities as in section A and maximizing total happiness as in section D is, first, a matter of degree—in the first case, feelings are an additional component of utility, in the second case, they are all that matters; and, second, that in the first approach individuals are still considered unitary, and revealed preferences still apply, whereas the second approach applies even when there are severe behavioral biases.

[4] In fact this position, though legitimate since many people would rationally elect not to have a negative feeling if they could, raises considerable intellectual difficulties. A tacit assumption in the standard economic framework is that only objective outcomes (i.e., outcomes that an outside observer would agree have occurred, such as consumption of a good or a service) are valued, not subjective ones. If one relaxes that assumption, as is needed to treat envy as an externality, then virtually all interactions are associated with externalities. See the discussion at the end of this chapter.

have several incarnations, as in the case of time inconsistency. People may then regret their own past choices, and a naive paternalist may see that as a case of people acting so as to harm themselves. But in fact these past choices were made by another incarnation; they harm my current incarnation but made my previous incarnation happier. Thus a paternalistic intervention does not "save the individual from himself" but instead should be viewed as redistributing between his various incarnations. This again raises the problem of knowing where this mandate comes from.[5]

Consider the example of undersaving. Due to hyperbolic discounting, I will be happy to commit to save \$1,000 next month. However, when next month comes, I will in fact prefer to consume \$1,000. A policy of forcing me to save that amount will make my current incarnation better off. But at the same time it will make my incarnation next month worse off. So the policy is enhancing my welfare at the expense of my next incarnation. How can one justify that "we" want to do that, without resorting to an arbitrary paternalistic statement that "we" have different tastes about the allocation of consumption between current and future incarnations than the current incarnation does?

One possible answer is that the government could be utilitarian in a redefined sense, by maximizing the sum of the utilities of all incarnations of all individuals rather than the sum of the utilities of all individuals. Thus the government could be willing to reduce my welfare now in exchange for an increase in the welfare of my old-age incarnation because initially that incarnation has a lower consumption level, and redistributing in its favor increases social welfare because its utility increases more than mine. More generally, as pointed out by Weyl (2009), any theory of justice or redistribution between individuals can be converted into a foundation for paternalism by applying it to the internal selves instead of the individual.

Indeed, a utilitarian social welfare function which counts each incarnation as a different individual will always put more weight on my future consumption relative to my current one than I do. This is because it enters into the social welfare function both "directly" through the contemporaneous future incarnation (with the weight of any incarnation) and indirectly through my own utility function (with my own weight on future consumption). Since the future incarnation, by definition, does not value my current consumption,[6] the total weight

---

[5] The issue of errors coming from, say, cognitive dissonance can arguably be viewed as a milder form of multiple incarnations. As long as the individual persists in his or her mistakes, there will be a difference between the "incarnation" that is acting and the one that is taken care of in the government's social objective. Mary, say, is taking that hazardous job. Studies show that people miscalculate the risks they are exposed to. They conclude that Mary's welfare is enhanced if such and such regulations are imposed on her workplace. But these regulations are costly and reduce her wage in equilibrium. Mary disagrees and would rather have a higher wage than those regulations that are supposed to enhance her welfare. Thus there is at least one definition of "Mary" whose welfare cannot be enhanced by the proposed policy, namely, the one who openly disagrees with it.

[6] This is, in fact, just an assumption. It is made throughout the literature and in our examples in chapter 4. However, we may conceive that we care about the welfare of our past selves, particu-

in the social welfare function of future consumption relative to current consumption is higher than mine. Therefore the social welfare function implies that, in the absence of redistribution, the future incarnation consumes too little; consequently, social welfare goes up if one redistributes from current incarnations to future ones. This can take place through a tax on the current income whose proceeds are invested into assets that will finance future consumption, which is roughly equivalent to a forced savings scheme. Furthermore, the argument does not rely on individuals being hyperbolic or time inconsistent but only derives from the assumption that the same individual has different selves at different points in time. Hyperbolic discounting just magnifies this problem by further reducing the current incarnation's weight on future consumption relative to that of the social planner, but the argument is essentially unchanged: what matters is that the same individual at different points in time is treated as a different person.

Alternatively, we may want to minimize the level of paternalistic intervention and refuse to allow the government to implement policies that redistribute between incarnations of the same person. Intervention would then be prescribed only if it made all incarnations better off, that is, only if it is Pareto improving.

C. The Pareto Criterion

The idea that policy could improve the welfare of all the incarnations of the same individual is intriguing. Most of the debate and most of the examples we have discussed revolve around the observation that there is a trade-off between the welfare of the short-run self and that of the long-run selves, which suggests that pleasing one harms the other. Is it possible that the behavioral biases also harm all the selves, so that we can increase welfare for each of them?

Consider a policy that would force me to consume less than I would otherwise consume. How can such a policy possibly benefit my current incarnation? This can only happen if the policy also changes the behavior of my future incarnations in a way that would benefit me. If the policy does not constrain their behavior, it must harm my current incarnation; otherwise, I would actually be willing to go ahead with the prescribed behavior, and I would not consume "too much" in the first place. On the other hand, if the policy constrains my future incarnations, it can compensate for the costs it is imposing on my current one. For example, I may be unhappy with how much I expect to consume next year, because I expect it will reduce the resources available to me in my old age. That is the essence of hyperbolic discounting: I know that my self next year puts more

---

larly through memories. Because the past is not affected by our current decisions, this would typically not affect our conclusions, but it does affect the point that a utilitarian social planner cares more about our future consumption relative to our current one than we do.

weight on my consumption next year relative to my old-age consumption than I do. Therefore a forced savings scheme that reduces consumption for both my current incarnation and my incarnation next year may increase my current incarnation's welfare if the increase in old-age consumption is large enough to compensate for the reduction in current consumption.

How about my self next year? It can also be made better off by the scheme. The reason is that because of the increased savings this year, it will inherit a greater level of wealth. To be sure, the policy constrains it to spend that wealth in old age rather than next year. But the increase in old-age consumption may again be enough to increase its total welfare on net.

As for my old-age self, it gains unambiguously, since it does not have any future period to provide for, and its consumption goes up.

Thus we see that one can find examples where a paternalistic policy makes all incarnations of the same individual better off. A numerical example is given in the appendix to this chapter.

The potential for Pareto-improving government intervention comes from the failure of trade between successive incarnations:[7] I cannot sign a contract with my future selves, as they do not coincide in time with my current self. Because of that, I cannot constrain their future behavior; conversely, they have no control on the environment they will face as a result of my current decisions. If I could bargain with them, we might reach a deal such that they would inherit from me a better environment (for example, I could save more and they would have more wealth) in exchange for making choices I like better. Absent trading between incarnations, the forced savings policy can be interpreted as an attempt to replicate the contracts that my successive incarnations would be happy to sign if only they could meet.

I want to tie my own hands to prevent my future incarnation from spending too much of the wealth I have left to it. Once it is that incarnation's turn to make a decision, the present is "salient" again and it wants to consume a substantial share of its wealth, thus reneging on the implicit contract. It is this problem that affords the government an opportunity to intervene in order to improve welfare. Forcing people to save a large enough fraction of their income acts as a commitment device for my future selves. The minimum savings provision indirectly implements a Pareto-improving contract between the two successive incarnations: my self next month is compelled not to consume too much of its wealth, which in turn makes me happy to bequeath more wealth than if commitment were not available.

All we have proved here is that there exists a kind of government intervention that restricts individual choice and works for *some* individuals, in the sense that the welfare of all their incarnations improves. This does not mean that these

---

[7] Again, this is just an assumption. That my future self is not experiencing a stream of utility right now does not mean that it is not currently available for bargains and transactions. This counterassumption underlies the Coasian critique of behavioral economics discussed in chapter 12.

interventions *should* be implemented. One shortcoming—the most relevant one—is that not all individuals need have multiple incarnations. There may exist individuals whose savings rate is quite low, not because their preferences are time inconsistent but because they have a high rate of time preference. The minimum savings rule, if it constrains these individuals to save more, will make them worse off than no rule at all. Thus the policy, despite being Pareto improving *within* inconsistent individuals, will not be Pareto improving across individuals; it redistributes welfare away from unitary individuals in favor of inconsistent individuals. Even individuals who are mildly inconsistent but have a high rate of time preference will find that the policy makes them worse off. We need a precise knowledge of each incarnation's utility to be able to improve the welfare of all incarnations. In the example in the appendix to this chapter, the Pareto-improving scheme must be precisely computed. For example, a 50 percent minimum savings requirement harms Incarnation 2, because it distorts its intertemporal consumption choices but does not bind Incarnation 1 to leave more wealth to Self 2 as a compensation.

▌ D. Aggregating Happiness

Since behavioral economics tells us that people have multiple selves so that they are not responsible for the consequences of their actions, and since happiness research proposes that policy should aim at making people feel good, it is only natural to expect the whole set of values underlying our society to shift away from a definition of welfare based on objective actions to a definition based on subjective feelings. This leads to the fourth solution to the social welfare problem: aggregating happiness rather than utility.

A traditional utilitarian wants to maximize the total sum of utility and considers utility to be based on revealed preferences, that is, the objective, observable actions of people. A post-utilitarian may instead want to maximize some total flow of happiness, for example, the total quantity of left-brain flashes or happiness hormones produced by the population. More realistically, however, one would again have to rely on self-reported, subjective feelings.

Under the new feelings-based notion of welfare, there is no obvious way to make my freedom compatible with your freedom, because it is always possible that what makes me feel good makes you feel bad, and vice versa. Consequently, there is no longer scope for such a thing as the first and second welfare theorems which tell us that we can design society and freedoms so that an efficient outcome is reached no matter what people want. To have any chance of maximizing my feelings-based utilitarian social welfare function, I need a great deal more intrusion in people's private lives: I need to measure the effect of my actions on my happiness and on the happiness of others. Then, once studies have been produced to elicit what makes people happy, policy can impose restrictions on people on the grounds that these restrictions increase total happiness. Clearly that was not needed with unitary rational individuals, because any action actually undertaken makes people happier than other feasible alternatives, and any voluntary transaction makes both parties better off. When revealed preferences are tossed out the window, Big Brother enters through the back door. Any individual action can be scrutinized and penalized on the grounds that it exerts some unwelcome externality on somebody else's feelings.

By contrast, any trade-off between two individuals' welfare was naturally solved, under the traditional liberal view, by introducing property rights. From the point of view of traditional economic theory, utility is derived from material goods. Most of these material goods are *excludable*, meaning that one may decide not to consume the good by simply not purchasing it, and that one prevents somebody else from consuming it by doing so oneself. When excludability fails (as in the case of air pollution), we are faced with an externality, and corrective taxes can potentially increase everybody's welfare. Absent that, markets work well and deliver a price that reflects the true value of the goods to those who use it. If, for example, this electric shaver irritates my skin, I will not be willing to pay a high price for it. If others do not have that problem they may bid the price up, and I may prefer to buy another shaver. If it irritates everybody, then either its equilibrium price must be low or the product will be driven out of the market. In all cases, either I am not irritated or I am compensated for this problem by a low price.

Most material goods are excludable, and this is partly why economists traditionally had a presumption in favor of private property and free markets. But that is not true of most of the *signals* people regularly exchange between them. If I come across ugly people in the street,[8] no market can prevent that.[9] The same holds if I hear comments that offend me, if I see people engaged in postures that I consider obscene, or if I pass a butcher's window with meat that makes me feel impure, or, indeed, if the very market signals we exchange in the course of our transactions—the prices—elicit negative emotions in my brain. Traditional economics was just dismissing those effects by defining a good in a "materialistic" way and having an "objective" definition of what an externality is. Thus there is a difference in nature between documented objective lung damage created by smoke emissions and a feeling of unhappiness. That is fortunate to the extent that excludability is the presumption for material goods, whereas nonexcludability is the presumption for signals—implying that externalities were considered the exception rather than the rule. But this difference is highly contingent on our ability to measure the first kind of effects (objective material damages) better than the second kind. The more neurosciences allow us to ob-

---

[8] This had been put to me by a heavy smoker as an argument in defense of his own external effects imposed on me.

[9] I could arguably bribe them—the "Coasian argument"—but if say I dislike 10 percent of the people I come across, that is going to be extremely costly; furthermore, I would have to write a fairly complex contract with each of these people that would specify which streets they are supposed to use and when, and that contract has to be enforced.

jectively measure happiness and stress by using brain scans and other means, the greater the scope for regulating the exchange of signals between individuals on the basis of their associated psychological "externalities," thus potentially curtailing freedom of speech, among other things. Note, however, that in principle even a post-utilitarian may refrain from going that way because, first, these offensive effects should not be defined by the "victim" but documented by some "study," and, second, the psychological benefits of the regulation to the potential recipients of offensive messages must be balanced by the psychological costs to the senders of their reduced freedom.

One proponent of using a post-utilitarian social welfare function defined as the total sum of happiness is Layard (2003). In his own words, "I want to propose the principle of greatest happiness." How, then, does one avoid the criticism that this may run against individual freedom even more than utilitarianism would? One answer is that people value freedom intrinsically because it makes them feel happy. This is indeed what the evidence discussed in chapter 5 shows. At least this argument has the merit of escaping consequentialism, since it opens the door for one allocation to be considered as better than an alternative one which yields the same material outcome, on the grounds that the former elicits better feelings than the latter. Going back to the example of the French CSG tax, we may now reject making the already paid CSG part of taxable income if it makes people furious. But we move from a paradigm where individual freedom is just a technique to decentralize the allocation that maximizes social welfare, until the day Lange's omniscient auctioneer replaces that imperfect instrument, to a paradigm where it is just a source of positive feelings and should be valued only to that extent, given the empirical evidence. In such a world, what really matters is feeling free rather than actually being free. And freedom competes on a level playing field with other sources such as job security or my neighbor being discrete about his latest achievements or, indeed, Prozac, which, from a post-utilitarian perspective, might achieve far better results than a set of outdated human rights. In the end we have made consequentialism worse by targeting subjective consequences in addition to objective ones.

This chapter has discussed the approaches that may replace strict utilitarianism when individuals are not unitary. The next chapter discusses in greater detail the actual policies that are advocated on the basis of behavioral and happiness research.

Appendix to Chapter 6

A Numerical Example

Suppose that at any date I enjoy a flow of utility from consumption, which is described in Table 6.1 (this utility function is concave).

Table 6.1. Utility as a Function of Consumption

Units of Consumption	Utility
1	7
2	13
3	18
4	21
5	23
6	25
7	26.5
8	28
9	29
10	30
11	31

Different incarnations weigh these utility flows differently; as the present is salient, Incarnation 2 puts more weight on its current utility at t = 2, relative to utility at t = 2 than does Incarnation 1. Table 6.2 defines the weights on these utility flows for each incarnation.

Table 6.2. The Weights on Utility

Incarnation\Date	t = 1	t = 2	t = 3
t = 1	1	0.5	0.5
t = 2		1	0.4
t = 3			1

We see that while Incarnation 1 is willing to trade utility one for one between the two future periods t = 2 and t = 3, Incarnation 2 wants 2.5 units of utility at t = 3 in exchange for a current reduction of one unit at t = 2. Suppose Self 1 has 20 units of consumption and that it can act as a dictator and allocate it once and for all between the three periods. It is easy to see that it will decide to consume 10 units at t = 1 and 5 units in the remaining two periods. Using Table 6.1, we can see that its total utility is then equal to $1 \times 30 + 0.5 \times 23 + 0.5 \times 23 = 53$. To implement that consumption plan, Incarnation 1 eats 10 units of consumption, leaves the remaining 10 to Incarnation 2, and instructs it to consume 5 and leave 5 to Incarnation 5.

What if there is no way to compel Incarnation 2 to obey these instructions? We can show that if left on its own with 10 units of consumption, it will not implement these instructions. That would give it a utility level equal to 1×23

+ 0.4 × 23 = 32.2. However, it is better off with consuming 7 now and 3 in the future, which leaves it with 1 × 26.5 + 0.4 × 18 = 33.7 units of utility. Self 1's original plan will therefore not be carried through. The original plan is not time consistent.

In this framework, the only failure of rationality is that people have multiple, inconsistent selves. But each incarnation is rational in that it maximizes its own well-defined utility and is able to perform computations and think through the consequences of its choices. Therefore Incarnation 1 will recognize that Incarnation 2 will not carry its plans through but instead will consume a larger fraction of the savings than originally intended, because it puts a lower weight on consumption at t = 3 relative to consumption at t = 2 than Self 1 does. If Incarnation 1 knows how its future selves behave, it is able to compute what will happen as a result of its choices today and how this affects its utility. This will generally lead to a different consumption choice at t = 1, which reflects the fact that Self 1 cannot trust its future incarnations. It turns out, however, that in our simple example, Self 1's optimal choice is still to consume 10 units and leave 10 to Self 2. The resulting utility level is therefore 33.7 for Self 2, and for Self 1 it is equal to 30 + 0.5 × 26.5 + 0.5 × 18 = 52.25, which is obviously lower than the 53 units of utility that Self 1 would get if it could constrain Self 2's future choices. This allocation is the "no commitment" or "time consistent" allocation: It is what we get if my current self cannot tie its hands and constrain the behavior of my future selves.

Now consider a government regulation that forces Self 2 to save at least 50 percent of its inherited wealth. That would compel it to consume 5 instead of 7, and will implement the optimal plan that Self 1 would want to carry through if it were a dictator. This regulation makes Self 1 better off, but it clearly harms Self 2, since it does not inherit more wealth and is forced to deviate from its optimal plan. However, let us now consider a regulation that forces Self 1 to save at least 11 units and Self 2 to save at least 5 units. This yields a utility level of 29 + 0.5 × 25 + 0.5 × 23 = 53 for Self 1, and 25 + 0.4 × 23 = 34.2 for Self 2. While Self 1 achieves almost[10] the same level of utility as if it were a dictator, and therefore is better off than under no commitment, Self 2 is also clearly better off than in the no commitment situation where its utility is 33.7. As for Self 3, it is also better off since it consumes 5 units instead of 3 in the no commitment case. We thus have an example of a Pareto-improving restriction on individual behavior: all selves are better off.

The Pareto-improving policy that we have considered imposes different savings requirements on each incarnation. In our example above, a uniform 51 percent savings requirement will also improve over no commitment. It would lead the individual to consume 9 at t = 1, 5 at t = 2, and 6 at t = 3. It would yield a

---

[10] That the numbers are identical is actually the result of our rounding; the utility is, in fact, slightly lower.

utility of $1 \times 23 + 0.4 \times 25 = 34$ to Self 2, which is still higher than the 33.7 it gets under no commitment, even though it is lower than what it would get under the non-uniform policy we have considered. Self 1 would get the same utility level of 53. But, again, one needs a precise knowledge of utility to compute the range of savings requirement that works. And no uniform policy may work in some cases.

7

The Policy Prescriptions of Behavioral Economics

Behavioral economics opens a whole new range of potential policy interventions and regulations. Traditional economics supports such regulations, as we have seen, provided there is a well-documented externality, or provided there are distributional concerns. In both cases, interventions should be as efficient as possible. This means using Pigovian taxes and subsidies for dealing with externalities, and transfers and income taxes for redistribution. In contrast, behavioral economics can justify restricting individual choices more directly, with the goal of preventing people from harming themselves, or harming others in a subjective way.

It should be emphasized that the drift toward paternalism is entirely consistent with the research program of traditional economics, which supposes that policies should be advocated on the basis of a consequentialist cost-benefit analysis, using some appropriate social welfare function. Paternalism then derives naturally from these premises, by simply adding empirical knowledge about how people actually behave: the worm was already in the fruit, as we saw in chapter 3.

It is worth reproducing how O'Donohue and Rabin (2003), two prominent contributors to the recent literature on behavioral economics, envisage a move toward paternalism:

> Economic policy prescriptions might change once we recognize that humans are humanly rational rather than superhumanly rational, and in particular it may be fruitful for economists to study the possible advantages of *paternalistic policies* that help people make better choices. We propose an approach for studying optimal paternalism that follows naturally from standard assumptions and methods of economic theory: Write down assumptions about the distribution of rational and irrational types of agents, about the available policy instruments, and about the government's information about agents, and then investigate which policies achieve the most efficient outcomes. In other words, economists ought to treat the analysis of optimal paternalism as a mechanism-design problem when some agents might be boundedly rational.

This sounds perfectly reasonable. The authors go on to argue that for econo-mists to matter they should get rid of their revealed-preference doctrine:

> Economists will and should be ignored if we continue to insist that it is axiomatic that constantly trading stocks or accumulating consumer debt or becoming a heroin addict must be optimal for the people doing these things merely because they have chosen to do it.

And, finally, they try to convince us that paternalism is not a big deal after all, because presumably it remains true that most people know better than the state what is good for themselves, so that scientists will surely find out and only de-sign a moderate dose of paternalism:

> Our approach therefore imposes a check against promiscuous paternal-ism by public or private entities. Most adults in most situations make better choices for themselves than others would make for them, and a careful study of optimal paternalism will surely reinforce many of the traditional economic arguments against paternalism.

But that is just a presumption, since only science can determine the optimal amount of paternalism:[1]

> Although even here our approach forces us to draw such conclusions through explicit analysis rather than a priori assumption.

So, what kind of policy prescriptions arise from the research in behavioral economics?

Restricting Choices for the People's Own Good

A frequent prescription, in various contexts, is to restrict people's choice set, (which falls in the category of strong paternalism). Consider biases in the way people process information. Akerlof and Dickens (1982) use a model of cogni-tive dissonance to argue in favor of mandatory safety standards at the work-place. That is because cognitive dissonance will prevent people who work in hazardous occupations from properly evaluating the risks involved. These work-ers are more likely to have entered these occupations with the prior knowledge that they are safe and will tend to discard news that contradict this knowledge. This will induce them not to behave cautiously enough in the work place. Aker-lof and Dickens advocate that regulation should be put in place so as to force

---

[1] Although the authors are concerned about real-world individual behavior, they do not seem to be bothered by real-world paternalism, for example, the fact that people who smoke at home cannot get a job at the World Health Organization or that policemen are routinely paid to spy on people inside their cars to check whether they have fastened their seat belt or are not using their mobile phone.

the workers to adopt the behavior that would be optimal, conditional on processing the information rationally. An example of such a policy would be to make it compulsory to wear a helmet on construction sites. Here we have an example where the behavioral bias is systematic, and a systematic policy is called to correct it.

Sheshinski (2002) and Saint-Paul (2002) show that if people make mistakes, and if the government knows both the distribution of mistakes and the distribution of preferences, then the government may sometimes increase total social welfare (in a utilitarian sense) by constraining individual choice. For example, if the government knows that, on average, the monetary equivalent of the utility derived from a good is between, say, $50 and $150, it knows that any transaction at $300 is likely to result from a mistake on the buyer's side. If mistakes are frequent enough, a completely rigid policy of imposing a price of $100 may be preferable to freedom of prices. Similarly, one may argue that under-saving for retirement is very likely to result from a mistaken evaluation of one's future needs, and accordingly impose a compulsory pension system. This is similar to Sheshinski's proposal.[2]

▍Taxation

The most compelling case for paternalistic intervention is that of higher taxes for addictive goods (so-called sin taxes). Such a tax reduces the current consumption of an addictive good by time-inconsistent consumers; this, in turn, reduces consumption of the good by consumers' future incarnations. Their welfare will increase if being addicted is associated with a loss of utility, that is, if the utility of my future incarnation depends negatively on the amount of the good consumed by my current one. As in the case of compulsory savings analyzed in chapter 6, this may, in principle, also increase the welfare of current incarnations by providing a commitment device.

The legitimacy of such a proposal comes from the fact that, as long as some public goods have to be financed, taxes are a necessary evil. Some optimal tax system must be designed so that it makes sense to embody what we know about behavioral biases in the design of taxation. Since taxes have to be paid anyway,

---

[2] My own contribution has been misunderstood by some reviewers as *advocating* such interventions, when all it was doing was in fact *analyzing* it, in a utilitarian context, which, as far as advocacy is concerned, I am in fact rejecting. Another part of the paper actually also discussed how the market could make intervention redundant by providing counseling that would help people overcome their own mistakes. Intellectuals, and notably economists, are all too often expected to be advocating some policy and enrolled in some project for "making the world a better place to live," often at the expense of disinterested research. This modern version of Benda's *trahison des clercs* is so deeply ingrained in today's culture that a journalist suggested to me that an economist who does not make policy prescriptions is simply useless. Obviously this presumption plays no small part in the rise of the paternalistic state.

one may argue that there is no less freedom under a paternalistic tax system that levies higher taxes on addictive goods than under a uniform tax system, if the paternalistic one has lower taxes on nonaddictive goods as a compensation. In terms of our earlier definition, sin taxes are weakly paternalistic and do not restrict individuals by channels other than the price system, which any other tax also does.

Of course, these alternative tax systems have different effects on different groups. But this is true of any system, and one cannot avoid weighing the net gains of one social group against those of another when designing taxes. Here the issue is that the sin tax would harm rational consumers who do not have commitment problems. These consumers would face an unbalanced tax structure which would lead them to consume too low a level of the addictive good, as any reasonable drinker who wants to buy some wine in a Swedish restaurant will painfully experience. More balanced taxation would even the distortions induced by taxes across goods and, this would increase the utility of these consumers. But one can nevertheless make a clever argument that _some sin tax is optimal._ The idea is that when an economic agent is in an optimal situation, it is harmed very little by being forced to deviate only slightly from that optimum. Suppose, for example, I am buying a car. My second-best choice is almost identical to my best choice; thus being forced to purchase my second-best choice has only a small effect on my welfare.[3]

What does that have to do with taxing addictive behavior? Consider a tax system that is optimal provided no consumer is time inconsistent. If there are time-inconsistent consumers in the economy, this tax system is not optimal for them, and they may have substantial gains from moving in the direction of sin taxes. On the other hand, initially, as the deviation from the optimum is small, rational consumers only have very small losses from moving toward sin taxes, by virtue of the preceding argument. Thus if there is some way in which the welfare of the two categories of consumers is aggregated, which is true for a utilitarian social planner, it must be that the irrational consumers gain more than the rational ones. Therefore some sin taxes are always optimal.

It may even be the case, furthermore, that everybody is better off, if the shift in the tax structure increases tax receipts. One can then give the rational consumers a rebate as compensation for the fact that they are paying too much for their cigarettes. In other words, the irrational consumers are bribing the rational ones for a tax system that allows them to solve their own commitment problems.

Thus we have a case where the possibility of Pareto improvement again arises. As with undersaving, we may ask whether the irrational consumers could find commitment devices of their own instead of being tamed by a tax system designed on the basis of their inconsistent behavior. O'Donohue and Rabin (2003) point out that one could improve the outcome even further by offering con-

---

[3] Technically the welfare objective that one is maximizing becomes very flat near the optimum.

sumers a *menu* of different tax schedules. The rational ones would choose the one with no additional taxes on the addictive goods. The irrational ones will be happy to sign up for a tax system that will tie their hands and prevent them from smoking. It is not totally clear how such a system could be implemented. One issue is that rational and irrational consumers could trade with each other on a secondary market in order to pay the lowest tax rate on each commodity: this would allow one incarnation of the irrational individuals to renege on the commitment made by another incarnation when it signed up for the scheme.

▌ Pricing Pseudo-Externalities

As we have discussed, happiness research states that people exert externalities on others' feelings and, if they have behavioral biases, fail to take into account their own habituation to different income and consumption standards. These effects imply that people will work too much and devote too little time to the activities that are not subject to habituation and rivalry. An extreme example is if people care about their rank relative to others. Any advance in the ranking must be met by somebody else's degradation. From a utilitarian viewpoint, the total sum of individual rankings is fixed. The ranking game is therefore a zero-sum game, and all effort spent on it is useless. From there, it is natural to advocate that rivalry should be priced by using Pigovian taxation.[4] Thus Layard (2003) states:

> So what is the appropriate level of taxation at the margin? [...] I have already suggested 30 percent to deal with rivalry, and the evidence suggests *at least* as much to deal with habituation. Thus 60 percent would not seem inappropriate, and that is in fact the typical level of marginal taxation in Europe [...] I suspect that in some almost unconscious way the electorate understand that the scramble to spend more is in some degree self-defeating and this makes them more favourable to public expenditure.

Such measures would of course reduce the GDP, but that is the whole point. Indeed, in the pure ranking game, all economic activity should be taxed at 100 percent. Ranking should be allocated on the basis of any effortless, exogenous achievement, or purely randomly.

It is not difficult to criticize such a proposal from a purely operational viewpoint. For example, the argument does not specify at which margin tax rates should be set at more than 60 percent, that is, the *average* level of taxation is not specified. It ignores the fact that, as we saw in chapter 6, all we need for the habituation effect to be internalized is to make people *aware* of it, and they can then refrain from increasing their living standards. Contrary to the undersavers,

---

[4] Equivalently, instead of formulating rivalry effects as an externality, one may formulate the frame of reference as a public good, to borrow from Frank's (1997) title.

they do not even need access to illiquid assets; they just have to refrain from buying that flashy car. So for the tax rate of more than 60 percent to be warranted, the electorate has to remain unconscious (Layard assumes that they are conscious of habituation when voting for a high marginal tax rate but not when making their consumption choices). Precisely how the incidence of a lower GDP will be distributed among people is not mentioned. What if a cardiologist decides that experts and studies are right, that it's stupid after all to buy a glossy Lamborghini, and dumps a few of his patients in order to take more time off with his family? How is the well-being of the patients affected? What if that entrepreneur who works seventy hours a week to gain market shares calls it a day and closes his factory? In a market society the pursuit of status and material achievement is obtained through voluntary exchange, and must thus benefit somebody else. Owning a Lamborghini is futile, but curing a heart disease is not. The cardiologist may be selfish and alienated; he makes his neighbors feel bad; and he is tired of the Lamborghini. His foolishness, however, has improved the lives of many people, even by the standards of happiness researchers. Competition to achieve status may be unpleasant to my future incarnations and those of my neighbors, but it increases the welfare of those who buy the goods I am producing to achieve this goal. In some cases, of course, status is achieved at the material expense of others, that is, it is not mediated by voluntary exchange but by nonprice competitive mechanisms such as rent seeking, lobbying, extortion, blocking entry, and so on. But then we are facing externalities and market failures in the traditional sense.

One should also take into account what is going to happen with the tax proceeds. If they are rebated to the people as a lump sum, wouldn't they spend it, thus making others feel bad? If we spend it on public goods, how do we know that these goods are not subject to habituation and thus not bringing more happiness than private goods? And what about the effect on happiness of being taxed? Chapter 6 has documented the role of loss aversion and endowment effects. Doesn't that mean that paying taxes should be associated with considerable pain?[5] The mere fact of having to fill a tax return every year makes me considerably unhappier than the sight of my neighbor's Porsche. Surely one has to consider the happiness effects of what the government does.

---

[5] This is outside the scope of this book, but I am always struck by how the policy advice that comes out of research is often cherry-picked in order to fit within an implicit, predefined "progressive" framework. Thus Easterlin finds that pure economic achievements have, at best, only transitory effects on reported happiness, whereas shocks to personal life like a divorce depress reported happiness permanently. He then goes on to argue in favor of some taxes that would constrain people to work less and devote more time to their personal life, but he refrains from arguing in favor of making divorce more costly or abolishing unilateral divorce. Similarly Layard finds strong rivalry effects and uses that to advocate high and progressive income taxes, but he fails to point out that ghettos and segregated neighborhoods redistribute in the "right" direction: they benefit the poor by reducing their income aspirations. If so, the emphasis on desegregating neighborhoods, a "progressive" social objective, is mistaken.

Another mystery is that if we need such high marginal tax rates to achieve happiness, why were people unhappy under communism? According to Inglehart and Klingemann (2000), Russians were feeling most miserable at the height of communism. Yet with a 100 percent tax rate and no pressure to perform, they should have been reasonably happy. True, they had few political and civil rights, but most people shouldn't care. Only a few plan to run a newspaper or engage in politics. In contrast, economic freedom is relevant to everybody—and the Russians did not like their lack of economic freedom one bit. It is possible that institutions that explicitly repress freedom make people unhappy per se (and this is consistent with the evidence we have discussed), while at the same time greater economic freedom in practice does not make them happier. That is why a post-utilitarian may advocate that one should not live in a communist country because studies show that communism makes people feel bad, whereas they remain happy with a more than 60 percent marginal tax rate and the associated reduction in the GDP, despite the fact that it would prevent many people from doing what they want to do, just like communism does.

Further issues arise if the happiness studies are misinterpreted. If rivalry is the sign of being frustrated because one has achieved less than one could, as I suggested in chapter 5, then being artificially forced to underperform by the tax system is unlikely to improve things; that others are equally prevented from succeeding will not bring me any relief.

Thus, using taxes to correct the drive for status on happiness considerations may be criticized on many pragmatic grounds. But all these issues can potentially be solved by careful analysis, and there is no conceptual barrier to eventually coming up with a full array of policies which will tax people for the negative feelings they impose on others. We may weigh the negative rivalry effects of human activity against its contribution to the well-being of the buyers. We may evaluate how people feel when paying taxes and then design taxes to be as painless as possible. We may promote formal freedoms that make people feel well and at the same time optimally repress their use in a more discrete way than totalitarian regimes did. As long as one accepts the post-utilitarian, feelings-based approach, designing intrusive policies that actually work is only a matter of time and effort. This is why one cannot believe in freedom and simultaneously accept that approach. Promoting laissez-faire on the grounds that post-utilitarian social engineering is poorly designed and replete with unforeseen perverse effects amounts to falling into the same trap as Hayek did in his controversy with Lange: accepting the ethical premises of post-utilitarianism and only challenging it on its implementation.

If one takes the view that all that matters is the total flow of happiness, then there is no reason for policy to show any respect for the integrity of the self. Thus it becomes acceptable for policy to manipulate people, if it can be shown that such manipulations make them feel better. And one may sometimes reach a similar conclusion if one just wants to solve behavioral problems.

▌ Manipulating the Context

The mildest form of manipulation, which Thaler and Sunstein (2003) have labeled "libertarian paternalism," occurs whenever the government, having decided which outcome is "good" for the people, fools them into making the "right" decision, not by restricting their choices but by framing their choice problem so as to favor the preferred outcome. The importance of context effects has been documented in chapter 4. Empirically it is known that workers will generally elect to contribute to a pension fund if that is the default option in the forms they must complete and that the enrollment rate into the fund will be much lower if the default option is nonparticipation.[6] So, given that people put themselves in future embarrassing situations by not saving enough, and given that their future misery will be a burden on "society," it just makes sense to present as the default option the course of action that will prevent those situations. Similarly, in a cafeteria, healthy food may be presented in a more conspicuous fashion than unhealthy food.

The approach is "libertarian," because it does not reduce the set of choices that people have. Specifically, it does not harm rational unitary individuals by forcing them to make choices they do not want to make. Furthermore, in some instances it must be that some option *must* be presented as the default. One cannot simply put all the food in the cafeteria in equally visible and accessible places; one must decide which kind of food will be more accessible. If "capitalists" artificially raise their profits by conspicuously displaying food that is appealing to children and fattening, at the expense of those children, surely the government must be improving things if it passes a law requiring that healthy items are made more visible than unhealthy items.

One appeal of such policies is that they are "no big deal." However, we must ask on what grounds the government should favor certain outcomes. In the preceding example, this amounts to favoring the individual's "virtuous" incarnations. In other cases, such manipulations redistribute between interest groups and are akin to propaganda. For example, Sunstein (1997) states that,

> in environmental regulation, it is possible to manipulate the reference point by insisting that policymakers are trying to "restore" water or air quality to its state at date X; a proposal to "improve" air or water quality from date Y may "code" quite differently. The restoration time matters a great deal to people's judgment.

This means that the way the regulation is presented will have an impact on its support in the population, and therefore on whether the regulation will go through. Therefore, by designing its campaign, the administration is able to favor some interest groups over others. In his example, Sunstein presumes that improving (or restoring) water quality is the preferred policy. On what grounds?

---

[6] These issues are discussed, for example, by Diamond (2005).

Consider a somewhat similar example. We have seen, in chapter 4, the existence of an endowment effect. This suggests that the way taxes are collected is not neutral. If income taxes are collected before the income is actually paid on a person's bank account, as when taxes are withheld or are paid by corporations (excise taxes, corporate taxes, payroll taxes, etc.), then no individual is "endowed" with the tax money prior to its payment. Compare this to a system where people first earn the money and then have to write a check to the government. Thus one may argue that the first technology is a more efficient way of levying taxes, happiness-wise, than the second. The problem is, however, that it is also not neutral in other dimensions. Since there is also an "availability" bias, the first technology makes it easier for the government to implement high taxes by making the cost of taxes to the tax payer less salient. By contrast, when writing a check to the government, people directly experience the quantity of goods and services they might have purchased with that money. Thus levying taxes in a way that makes them easier to accept also favors a political agenda of bigger government.

Awareness

Perhaps the least objectionable "libertarian" paternalism consists in educating people about their own biases or about the objective reality they supposedly misperceive, or both. Like context manipulation, this approach does not strongly favor one outcome over another and would be neutral for rational individuals. A number of libertarian paternalists point out that biases are hardwired, and therefore coercing people into the "right" behavior would impose high psychological costs. Promoting awareness has no such problem, however, and would help those who are willing to exert self-control so as to benefit their long-term self. Arguably this is not paternalism, although the question remains as to why this particular information should be provided by the government rather than by private communication media. Indeed, the self-help literature is a flourishing one.

Manipulating Beliefs

Standard economic theory predicts that one is always better off if better informed. An improvement in the quality of information is somewhat similar to an increase in the number of options. A rational utility maximizer can always do at least as well with more information as with less information, by simply discarding the extra information and taking the same course of action.

Behavioral economics opens the door for restricting people's access to information for their own good. However, different psychological phenomena lead to different, potentially conflicting, policy conclusions. If we consider the cognitive biases independently of other biases, we observe both overconfidence and rationalization of past decisions. It would then be natural for a paternalistic government to offset them by overemphasizing the negative in order to restore a balance in people's subjective distribution of feelings. That resembles, to a degree, what is observed in campaigns about AIDS, smoking, or road safety, all of which aim at building "awareness" by "striking the minds." On the other hand, the confidence-enhanced performance view suggests that perhaps the government should suppress information so that people would be even more biased when estimating their chances of success (hence, perhaps, the practice of promoting self-esteem in many modern institutions). But this contradicts the happiness literature which would tend to predict that this would boost "aspirations" and make people unhappy when they are disappointed by their results. This contradiction is presumably owing to the fact that performance and happiness are two different things.[7] Also, there is a contradiction between manipulating information and increasing awareness of one's behavioral problems.

It is not my purpose to solve these contradictions here. Instead, I want to stress the point that the case for paternalistic intervention is somewhat stronger when cognitive dissonance prevails than with time-consistency problems. Assume, as emphasized by the literature on confidence-enhanced performance, that people who manage to fool themselves into believing that they can be high achievers indeed perform better. While hyperbolic discounters can constrain their future selves by signing long-term contracts, thus not needing government intervention, it is far more difficult for these people to actually fool themselves on purpose. They could pay a third party to insulate them from the outside world and report only good news to them; only a few people, however, would have access to such a technology, and, most important, as long as they know they are lied to, they will not believe the distorted information, and thus their attempt at manipulating their own beliefs will fail.

From there it is not difficult to advocate that governments should propagate false information in order to improve the context in which people make their decisions. The above-mentioned contradictions are an important obstacle, since we do not really know what the government should do, but if some day "science" agrees about which biases make people more efficient or happier, then it will have "proved" that manipulating information improves welfare. And it will be essential that these manipulations remain secret for this scheme to work; otherwise people will see through them and they will fail to boost their confidence (or happiness).

Note, however, that it is not clear how such instruments should interact with more traditional ones like sin taxes. If a sin tax is set optimally so as to deter

---

[7] To my knowledge, there are no attempts in the behavioral literature to put together all the phenomena that have been proposed and evaluate their consistency. Also, the psychological studies on which it draws are rarely challenged, which stands in contrast with the extreme scrutiny with which economists greet empirical studies in their own field, where no source of bias, measurement error, or reverse causality is ignored.

smoking, is any further intervention necessary? The research so far is largely silent on that issue, and by virtue of its consequentialism it has no presumption that manipulation is "wrong" compared to taxation; the answer only depends on how many instruments are needed to fine-tune the optimal outcome.

Manipulating Preferences

One important aspect of traditional economic theory is that preferences are taken as given: we consider a fixed set of individuals, each with his or her own well-defined utility function, and we simply ignore where that utility comes from. We then base policy on some aggregate of those utility functions across individuals. This approach makes sense if we consider a given policy proposal at a point in time, when the set of individuals comprising society is well defined. But it ignores the fact that preferences are inherited, not only through our genes but through the way we are raised by our parents.[8] Presumably, to the extent that parents can choose their children's preferences, they will do so in such a way as to maximize their own welfare. But we have no result that tells us whether this is a good thing or a bad thing from the point of view of the children. It is impossible, in fact, to establish such a result, for one needs a criterion for comparing alternative utility functions; that is, one would have to impose some "meta-utility function" in order to tell us that a given utility function is better than another. And there is no way such a meta-utility function can be derived from the child's preferences, since those are determined by the parents. If I am socialized to like chocolate, I am better off with that candy than without; if I had been socialized differently, however, I might have preferred something else instead, and I have no way to tell which of these two alternative socializations I prefer. My current self likes chocolate and prefers its own consumption basket to the one that my alternative self would have consumed, and vice versa. Each of my potential socializations is better off with its own consumption basket than with the others'.

On the other hand, economic theory does not suppose that preferences as inherited by parents are more legitimate than if they came from any other source. The theory does not preclude abducting children from some families to have them raised by other families. That would lead to the production of a different human being. The original family would lose if such a policy is implemented against its will. The foster family would gain. Whether the child would gain or lose is impossible to determine, since he would be two different individuals. The rest of society might gain or lose depending on the inputs supplied by the resulting individual to the markets, and on potential externalities he may or may not exert upon society. Suppose, for example, that children of disadvantaged parents are more likely to commit crime. Then removing them from their families and having them raised by families that are better off would reduce the

---

[8] See Bisin and Verdier 2000.

crime rate and impose a positive externality on the rest of society. We could similarly envisage children being bred in some collective youth organizations that would produce a different brand of human beings than families would. Utilitarianism, in principle, has nothing to say about whether such moves are desirable, since it does not allow us to compare the welfare of two societies made of different individuals. That is the only safeguard that economic theory has to offer against it: that it has nothing to say about its consequences on social welfare. But it could actually be twisted just a bit to validate these intrusive policies. For this we just need to allow ourselves to compare utility between two alternative versions of the same individual that cannot coexist in the same world. That is not much more far-fetched than comparing utility between two existing individuals, as utilitarianism routinely does. We could, in fact, justify it by invoking the usual veil-of-ignorance argument: before knowing who he is, wouldn't the individual prefer to be raised in a wealthy, stable family than in a dysfunctional one? So if we replace the individual's utility by another one that is larger, and if, in addition, the utility of the rest of society goes up because the individual exerts fewer negative externalities on it, we have built a case for removing children from their low-quality biological families and have them raised in higher-quality families or in collective youth organizations: that increases our measure of total welfare.[9] Although such radical solutions are not uncommon, they only affect a minority of households, those that typically are welfare-dependent. In a milder fashion, however, these arguments open the door for government to intrude in the social transmission of preferences through schooling, advertising, and the manipulation of information.

Thus the assumption that there are endogenous preferences further weakens the case for limited government embodied in welfare theorems. The only intellectual safeguard remaining is the above case that changing preferences cannot be Pareto improving. Even that no longer holds, however, if we move to a post-utilitarian social welfare function, at least in the version where the aggregate stream of happiness is being maximized. It then becomes perfectly legitimate to manipulate individual preferences so as to make people feel good. This is, in fact, what Huxley's *brave new world* society does. There, people are conditioned at an early age to feel good about the fate that the social planner has decided for them. This is done by using recorded messages that are repeated to them many times during their sleep. Consequently, the alphas are quite happy to be the executives that make the decisions, and are similarly happy about their access to some exclusive leisure activities. The betas are similarly happy to escape the stress and responsibility of the alphas, and find the alpha leisure activities quite boring. At the bottom of society, armies of clones who perform very menial jobs can hardly be made happy about it, so the central planner endows these

---

[9] One could even argue that society could compensate the original biological family by some monetary transfer, so that we would have proved that everybody is made better off by trading their children! Similarly, the original family could sell their child to the new foster family.

people with substandard mental abilities that make them incapable of either feeling something or reflecting on their own conditions. Finally, both the alphas and the betas have a deep fear of growing old and experiencing the associated diseases, so they are quite happy to be programmed to die at sixty. And the social planner is quite happy, too, since that saves on scarce resources.

We are not yet there. However, the post-utilitarian perspective may be used to promote a change in the contents of educational curricula. From a utilitarian point of view, education is a good like the others. Depending on the use one makes of it, it can be a consumption good (the "joy" of learning) or an investment good (accumulating human capital). For this reason, despite the fact that public educational systems are pervasive, the economic case for public provision of education is not very strong. It is reasonable to argue that education is associated with externalities—for example, having an extended vocabulary is more valuable if more people understand those words. However, that is a case for subsidization of education, not for public provision. Historically curricula have insisted on substantial contents ("knowledge") but have also taught non-cognitive skills that were meant to train "good citizens" (quite often, this meant aptitude to work), and they have not been free of political propaganda (for example, French history textbooks from 1870 to 1914 were promoting the goal of reconquering Alsace and Lorraine). Thus education has never been only a purely objective provision of human capital; it has also been a way for the elite to affect the culture, values, and beliefs of the people. This bias is likely to be reinforced if one thinks that educational systems should reflect the goal of producing happiness. Thus Layard (2007) outlines a program for using school curriculum to teach pupils how to be happy: "If *we* want to *change the culture,* the main organised institutions *we* have under *social control* are schools." The general premise is that the level of happiness can be targeted by public policies, because scientific studies help us understand its determinants—the existence of those studies and their scientific character justify the use of happiness as a criterion for designing curricula: "Only *science* can and should persuade the young about the routes to a happy society." By science, Layard does not refer to the objective natural sciences that led to such inventions as air travel or vaccination. Rather, "we have in positive psychology a science that provides the underpinning for morality and personal liberation." That does not mean, of course, that positive psychology should be taught, just that it should be used to determine the optimal massage of the children's neurones that will trigger the largest total flow of good feelings. The only difference with Huxley's novel (where positive psychology has proved that conditioning at an early age works, and is therefore used by "we" in the production of human beings) is that in the brave new world feelings are instrumental in maintaining a rigid social order; here, they are the goal being pursued.

What does "positive psychology" say about what should be done to the children so as to enhance their happiness? There seem to be two dimensions to it: therapy and values.

Let us start with the therapy. Layard advocates program such as the so-called Penn Resiliency Project: "In it, 15 11-year old students spend 18 classroom hours on such issues as understanding their own emotions and those of others." According to an evaluation study, the program has reduced the rate of teenage depression in subsequent years. Such prescriptions illustrate the radical change in paradigm associated with post-utilitarianism. They implicitly assume that happiness is one of the goals of the school system, as opposed to being a private matter; that social science can rigorously identify the sources of happiness and design the technology that produces it in the minds of children; and that the success of a technique in reducing depression, namely, treating a pathology, can be extrapolated to conclude that it is useful for enhancing everyone's happiness.

The other aspect of education is that it should teach "values." Of course, the values that one is promoting reflect one's conceptions about the individual and society. In the past, values were not supposed to make people happy. In most cases they consisted of taboos and prohibitions that constrained them, presumably making people unhappy when they were binding. Nor were values individualistic—they were supposed to buttress society and its institutions. Individuals benefited to the extent that some reciprocity is generated by the values, as in the case, say, of prohibiting theft, but in many cases the values implied self-sacrifice. With the enlightened liberal society described in chapter 1, values became more individualistic and were based on free will and responsibility. And this new set of values could conflict with the older set that sustained the community, as witnessed by episodes in American history such as the Civil War (when the cohesion of a community living on a slavery economy conflicted with human rights) or McCarthyism (when freedom of speech was thought to be a threat to national security). We naturally expect post-utilitarianism to promote different values, among them happiness defined as a feeling. This hardly qualifies as a moral system: if it were found, say, that victims of sexual abuse somehow enjoyed it (and we cannot presume they didn't on the grounds that this was not consensual, since we no longer believe in revealed preferences), then perhaps one should change the values taught at school and promote the view that such abuses should be welcome. It turns out, however, that the values which seemingly make people happy are not so provocative and somewhat resemble conventional ones. So, to quote Layard:

> If you care more about other people relative to yourself, you are more likely to be happy. [...] If you constantly compare yourself with other people, you are less likely to be happy. [...] Choose goals that stretch you, but are attainable with high probability. Challenge your negative thoughts, and focus on the positive aspects of your character and situation.

That is arguably a reasonable philosophy of life, and in old-fashioned curricula we were exposed to a variety of such philosophies—Stoicism, Epicurism, Confucianism. But these were just proposals, that is, a menu of attitudes toward life from which one were free to choose, whereas we are now in a situation where "science" defines which attitude is most efficient in producing happiness, and consequently should be taught.

One issue is that this presumes too much of the "science of happiness." For example, what if some conceptions are hardwired by evolution? How can one hope to change them by teaching different values? Would insisting on that not generate pathologies and eventually lead to failure? Also, the objective consequences of the proposal are ignored. If one discards negative thoughts, does that not reinforce the process of cognitive dissonance and likely lead people to make poor decisions? Should one then implement further restrictions to individual choice in order to counteract the inefficient decisions made by people trained in that way? If I am trained to be an altruist, isn't my happiness vulnerable to degradations in the status of the people whom I care about, in addition to my own status? And how can we make the preferences of altruistic people consistent with one another? How can A make B happy if B mostly cares about C's welfare, and so on? Shouldn't A know the utility of a lot of people in order to figure out what he should do to make B happy, taking into account the whole nexus of altruistic links between individuals?

Another problem with this positivist approach is that the state ends up being the key producer of values that are reduced to a morally neutral input into a (post) utilitarian social welfare function. There is no outside system of values to restrict the scope of state intervention, as long as it is established that those interventions increase the total level of happiness. And since revealed preferences no longer hold, only scientists can be trusted to establish that the happiness level has increased; the word of the people whom "we" are supposed to make happier is worthless. This stands in sharp contrast to the traditional liberal/Lockean view, where values should not be imposed by the state upon individuals. There, the state is just an agent in charge of a number of activities determined by people's preferences and values. It has no mandate to change these values.

To illustrate the potentially far-reaching consequences of such conceptions, let us consider the role of parental authority. Traditionally parental authority was unchallenged, because the family was one of the "values" upon which society was constructed. Clearly this can no longer be warranted if values are reduced to a mental input in the production of happiness.[10] Parents, then, are only valued provided they do the right thing. Perhaps children value their parents insofar as they are happy with them; but if that is not the case, or if parents make educational decisions that "science" has proved would make their children unhappy, then it is again quite defensible to remove children from their families. It all boils down to a cost-benefit analysis that weighs the foregone happiness from being separated from one's parents from the gain in happiness from being

---

[10] Whether the family is valued in the liberal utilitarian view is also far from obvious. For example, the intrusion of the state in the way children are raised can increase total utility whether or not it reflects feelings.

taught the right values and undergoing the right state-mandated therapy based on "positive psychology."[11]

If one pushes the goal of maximizing the total flow of happiness to its extreme, one may want to act upon feelings directly by the use of psychotropes. In Huxley's novel, people regularly use "Soma"; one may similarly use Prozac to produce positive feelings upon demand. For a pure feelings-based post-utilitarian, this would make all the other policies we have discussed useless; the only question is whether Prozac should be subsidized or even mandated, given the presumption that people fail to correctly anticipate the effects of their actions on their own happiness.

If happiness can be engineered by producing the appropriate chemicals in the brain, any notion of an individual, as defined by consciousness, free will, and responsibility, disappears. In the end there will be no reason to respect the lives of those organisms whose sole purpose is to host those chemical reactions.

Moral Hazard and Paternalism

In chapter 3 we have seen that the standard utilitarian approach does not support the view that public policy should restrain individual actions on the grounds that these actions have negative effects on society, for example through their effects on welfare dependency. We have argued, instead, that people should be free to pursue the course of actions they wish, but that the terms of their contract with "society" should be contingent on those actions; we have discussed how dynamic social contracting theory has provided foundations for that view in a utilitarian context.

In a post-utilitarian world, however, the self that is being punished for putting himself voluntarily out of jobs by not receiving unemployment benefits, or into indigence by not saving enough in the past, is not the same person as the one who did these harmful things in the past. He is instead suffering from an "externality" imposed on him by the decisions of his own past incarnation.[12] Isn't it just fair that social insurance covers such an adverse shock? If my past

---

[11] Layard says that "parents of course are crucial," but he does not tell us how he would handle parents who would produce unhappy children who, say, care too much about their relative status. Ironically, though, if these parents are few, their children would thrive and achieve a higher status than the others who do not care about status so that everybody would be happy about their fate just as in Huxley's novel. In fact, the children of these elite families who escape the happiness-driven school curriculum proposed by Layard might even end up being happier than the others, thanks to their superior relative status. Furthermore, this elite would be more than happy to promote the selfless happiness-based curriculum for others while making sure that their own children escape it and inherit a taste for relative success instead.

[12] Most of the argument being made here would carry through if instead of multiple selves there were unitary individuals but the government would be subjected to its own commitment problems that would preclude conditioning transfers on past behavior. An alternative policy prescription, however, would be an institutional reform that would eliminate this commitment problem.

self is different from my current self, there is no difference, from the point of view of my current self, between that situation and having lost one's job involuntarily because of the boss's decision to close the plant. In both cases my situation is the result of somebody else's decision. And if fairness means that the current self should be compensated by the welfare state, past decisions by my previous self also impose a "fiscal externality" on the tax payer. As we have seen, this fairness argument can be embodied in a post-utilitarian social welfare function through the extra weight given to future consumption by the social planner, in addition to its weight in the current incarnation. This extra weight reflects the fact that the extra incarnation is treated as a separate individual. It implies that any incentive scheme that penalizes current behavior by reducing the utility of some future incarnation will, in fact, harm the social welfare function *more* than it harms the individual. This makes it more problematic to use the schemes proposed by "dynamic social contracting theory": imposing ever-increasing penalties to people who repeatedly rely upon social insurance. This worked because the social cost of the penalties (i.e., their effect on the social welfare function) was entirely taken into account by the individual when deciding whether to rely on social insurance in a given period. When, instead, people have multiple incarnations, by pursuing dynamic incentive schemes, the social planner is now shooting himself in the foot; the social cost of these schemes now includes the harm done to the future incarnations. That part is not taken into account by the current incarnations, and therefore the total cost of punishment is larger than if the social planner were strictly utilitarian. Farhi and Werning (2005) in a similar context show that treating future selves as separate puts severe bounds on the degree of inequality that the social planner is willing to tolerate to induce incentives.

An important consequence is that in order to solve the moral hazard problem, it is now more valuable to rely on preventive paternalistic polices rather than incentive schemes relying on future punishment.

Intuitively the argument is as follows. Assume that the government has to elect one of two social insurance policies. Ignore the fact that the policy may deter work and job search and focus on the incentives to save versus to consume. Under the "incentive" plan, people can draw benefits when they are in need, but this reduces their future benefit levels should they be in need again. This is the type of policies prescribed by dynamic social contracting theory. Undersaving is deterred by the prospects of low future benefits. Under the "paternalistic" plan, everybody is entitled to the same level of benefits regardless of past behavior. But everybody is forced to save a minimal fraction of their income in order to prevent improvidence.

What are the trade-offs the policy maker faces when electing between the two schemes? The forced savings scheme reduces the welfare of those who (even in the absence of social insurance) would prefer to consume more now than their prescribed level. The incentive plan only provides incomplete insurance: those who have been unlucky so as to be hit repeatedly by adverse shocks are made poorer. Imperfect insurance is the price to be paid for implementing incentives. Incentives work because people realize that they will be harmed in the future if they draw too many benefits now.

Assume that the social planner treats individuals as unitary. To fix ideas, let us think of him as a standard utilitarian who is adding the welfare of all individuals. Then the fact that a given individual only has imperfect insurance reduces social welfare by the same amount as it reduces the individual's welfare. What happens if, instead, individuals are considered as having multiple selves? If I decide to draw more benefits today, this will reduce my future welfare. The social planner considers this cost, but he also considers that this is a cost to my future incarnation. In other words, the harm is counted once in my computations but twice in the social planner's computations because my future consumption is also the current consumption of my future incarnation. That is, the reduced welfare of my future selves is now similar to an externality that my current self is imposing upon it by drawing more benefits, and the future punishments should be made even higher to take that into account, but doing so would further reduce the insurance level associated with the incentive scheme, thus making it less valuable relative to the paternalistic one. Therefore it is more likely that the paternalistic plan is chosen if people are treated as having multiple selves.

This explains why we observe that modern welfare states are increasingly reluctant to deny benefits to individuals who put themselves in welfare dependency out of their own choice and instead prefer to rely on coercive preventive measures. Thus we see unconditional social assistance coupled with compulsory contributions to pension systems; taxes on tobacco and the proposal of a tax on "junk food," but free medical treatment of the associated subsequent health problems; and free delivery of heroin (or methadone) and needles to addicts, while its consumption is illegal for nonaddicts. The latter case is an example of a good being taxed for some individuals and subsidized for other individuals. This involves both a contradiction and inequality before the law (although the latter is only relative, since anybody can decide to become a drug addict and benefit from the subsidy).

Giving In: Paternalism as Demagogy

Although so far we have mostly considered policies that aim to impose the "right" behavior on the individual, instead the government could adapt itself to the public's biases. Salanié and Treich (2007) argue that taking those biases into account could lead governments to knowingly pursue objectively inefficient policies. The authors give the example of a city where most residents are wrongly convinced that tap water is contaminated. Such a belief results in costly consumption of, say, bottled water. The government then contemplates an investment which, it claims, reduces the content of pollutant X in tap water. Since X is already at totally innocuous concentrations, the investment would be a pure waste should consumers be rational. However, because of the consumers' misperceptions, it is actually socially profitable to implement the investment if it triggers a shift away from bottled water in favor of tap water, as long as the cost of the investment is lower than the additional cost of drinking bottled water instead of tap water.

There are many issues associated with such a prescription. To begin with, the investment is reinforcing the public's erroneous belief. If I observe the government taking costly security measures, I infer that it was correct for me to be worried. Indeed, a rational consumer who is not totally informed would make that inference, and the bias would be further reinforced by cognitive dissonance. Second, the argument implies that the cost-benefit analysis for public policy should be conducted on the basis of the people's subjective beliefs rather than objective information. How this might be pursued in practice is unclear; although objective cost-benefit analysis can be implemented by estimating the consumer demand for the project we are considering, factoring in subjective aspects seems far less doable. Third, as further discussed in chapter 10, a costly investment is probably dominated by manipulating the information of the people so as to convince them not to undertake the costly actions. Hence, if we could pretend that pollutant X is entirely absent from tap water instead of releasing its true concentration, we would save the cost of abating it and obtain the same result (a similar result would be obtained by pretending that bottled water is contaminated). But such manipulation is doable only to the extent that the government has some monopoly on information, and that is not always feasible. In our example, anybody can measure the concentration of X for themselves and make it public.

It is notable that, here, paternalistic policies arise because the state only has partial control over individuals. If it could force people to have correct perceptions, it could do away with the investment and would have no incentives to distort information. This partial control stems, among other things, from the fact that beliefs are affected by agents other than the state, specifically interest groups. Thus, in the precedent example, people could overestimate the risks associated with pollutant X because of propaganda by environmental protection groups (to which producers of bottled water may want to donate).

Positive Rights

The traditional liberal society rules out positive rights, because they constitute an infringement of somebody else's right. Even a utilitarian partisan of income redistribution would contend that the only positive right that should be granted is the right to social income assistance. By contrast, post-utilitarian approaches pave the way for far-reaching positive rights.

There are some naive justifications for positive rights that do not depend on behavioral biases. People may be considered as "victims of society" so that their deeds are presented as a form of compensation. Harming people who are viewed as weaker could cause negative public opinion. All these considerations, however, are a case for monetary compensation and not any other form of entitlement. The multiple selves approach, on the other hand, implies that people are entitled to more than social income assistance, since they are not accountable for the way that assistance is spent—the self who suffers from poor nutrition or poor housing is different from the one who spent the assistance money on, say, drugs. Thus social assistance can now take the form of a direct right to consume specific goods such as housing, food, transportation, or clothing, with the corresponding obligations to the providers, whether public or private. It is because of its increasing distrust for the individual's capacity to act rationally that our society is keen on positive rights.

Under feelings-based ethics, the ultimate positive right is the right to "feel good." Such a right may severely curtail individual freedom, since any form of communication between humans generates feelings and may consequently be regulated. Ultimately any individual can arbitrarily define his or her own rights on the basis of what makes that person feel good or bad. Take, for example, the right not to be offended by "hate speech" (often defined arbitrarily), so often promoted by politicians and the modern media. The traditional liberal view is that there is no such right, for if there were, the constitutionally granted right to freedom of speech would be violated. But suppose a "study has shown" that some kind of speech triggers bad feelings (for example, right brain flashes) in the people who listen to it, while having no noticeable effect on the happiness of those who speak? This can be used as a basis for censorship, since censoring that kind of expression would indeed increase the total amount of good feelings in the population.

How the generalization of such a right can overwhelm society is easily extrapolated. Whether individual responsibility should apply now depends on exogenous considerations. The rule of law now suffers exceptions and only applies conditionally. A given action is acceptable or not depending on whether the person who performs it is worthy of our compassion, depending on whether the circumstances create acceptable excuses, and so on. One, then, may well consider being rude or having made an offensive comment as a more serious crime than physically beating an individual. A crime no longer is defined as a violation of an objective limit set by the law but instead by the feelings of the "victim." Volokh (1997) describes how far this has gone in the United States in the area of workplace harassment jurisprudence:

> At the University of Nebraska at Lincoln, a harassment complaint was filed against a graduate student who had on his desk a 5" × 7" photograph of his wife in a bikini. The employer ordered that the photo be removed. [...] One court, for instance, has ordered an employer and its employees to "refrain from any racial, religious, ethnic, or other remarks or slurs contrary to their fellow employees' religious beliefs."

8

The Modern Paternalistic State

The preceding chapters have discussed how policy prescriptions can be derived from the post-utilitarian view. The present chapter initiates a journey through modern paternalism. Through a number of examples, we shall investigate its logic, or lack thereof, and relate it to the intellectual apparatus we have analyzed. An important point here is that only a fraction of the paternalistic interventions that we observe are grounded on the intellectual apparatus described in the preceding chapters. Conversely, many proponents of behavioral economics are in favor of a moderate dose of paternalism and would not approve of all the policies that we shall discuss. But this does not invalidate the point that by becoming behavioral, economics is no longer capable of providing an intellectual safeguard against excess government intrusion in private matters.

The paternalistic state has naturally evolved, in part, from the welfare state. As the poor were paid by the government, the government had the ability to ask for something in exchange and hence monitor poor people's behavior. This was also true of the alternative redistributive institutions, such as the family and the church. In principle, this should not be an issue: as long as one can "opt out" of redistribution, people who object to the paternalistic constraints imposed on them can simply forfeit the associated transfers. But the story becomes entirely different if, by making such a choice, I am now harming some of my incarnations. This opens the door for preventing me from opting out, and thus for the transformation of the welfare state into a paternalistic one.

Given these origins, the paternalistic state retains many elements of the welfare state. Its concern for equality, however, now takes place in a context where people have multiple incarnations, where some people are more rational than others, and where the objective is to maximize a flow of happiness. In other words, the objectives are broadly the same as those of the welfare state. But the paternalistic state needs far more regulations and interventions than the welfare state since it cannot rely on revealed preferences.

This relative impotence allows for numerous challenges and contradictions, which, far from being a case for a low profile, have in fact opened the door for wide-ranging government involvement in private matters. Let us discuss these challenges.

▌ The Dilemma between Prevention versus Repression

The first challenge is the dilemma between prevention and repression. The paternalistic state cannot rely on individual responsibility to enforce rules and private contracts, and is therefore reluctant to impose penalties on individuals for having breached the law or the contracts they have signed. Imposing a penalty is inherently unfair in a world of multiple selves: the incarnation that suffers from the penalty (say, is sent to jail) is different from the one that perpetrated the corresponding deed. Furthermore, penalties are less efficient in providing incentives. There is no way that Dr. Jekyll can prevent the criminal actions of Mr. Hyde, other than asking a third party to physically impede him from acting when he turns into his alternative incarnation. In conceptions of multiple selves less extreme than in Stevenson's novel, such as the theory of "hyperbolic" discounting we have seen, people have a high discount rate between today and tomorrow which leads them to act compulsively and largely disregard the consequences of their actions. Although this is not inefficient for a rational individual with a high rate of time preference but no hyperbolic discounting—he is just willingly sacrificing future utility in exchange for current utility, which he values much more—it is a case in favor of interventions as long as such impatient behavior is interpreted as harming future incarnations.[1]

In order to counteract those tendencies, it would be natural for the government to increase the penalties on future adverse consequences so as to offset the effect of the inefficiently low weight that the individual puts on the future. This seems to call for more repression. If Dr. Jekyll knew that Mr. Hyde would be hanged, he would immediately pay a third party to lock him in his house every night. Indeed, there is a trend toward greater penalties in some areas, such as sexual offenses. Yet greater penalties are costly, and the more short-sighted, uncommitted, and compulsive the individual to be deterred is, the greater the necessary penalty. The costs include direct costs such as those of administering prisons and indirect costs like the adverse effects on the incentive structure for criminals—if rape gets you thirty years in jail, why not go directly for murder instead? So there is also a sense that penalties do not work; one may then opt for alternative tools to achieve the desired outcome, notably "prevention." This tension is familiar to economists: when the cost of a resource goes up, we need to spend more on that resource (the "income" effect), but we are also more willing to use it less if an alternative exists (the "substitution" effect). In principle, where to go is determined by a cost-benefit analysis; in practice, this tension explains why we see greater penalties in some areas and lower penalties in others.

---

[1] While hyperbolic—or nonexponential—discounting is the typical justification for paternalistic government intervention in the literature, problems start arising as soon as the individual has multiple incarnations, which is not incompatible with exponential discounting. In other words, the individual's preferences may be such that his future incarnations will not want to revise his plans, yet one will give greater weight to future utility than the current incarnation by treating future incarnations as separate individuals.

When it comes to private contracts, nonenforcement may be the preferred course of public authorities; since there is no longer a presumption that the private contract is mutually beneficial, a court can decide that it is harmful to one party's incarnation and therefore void. Traditionally private contracts have always been void if one party was not in possession of its means when signing it. This reflected a recognition that judgment could be altered in some circumstances. In the behavioral era, however, this is almost always true by definition, because one individual's incarnation does not take into account the interests of the other incarnations at the time of signing the contract; those incarnations, moreover, are located in the same organism, and so there is no way one can insulate them from the clauses of the contract. Thus any contract involves third parties that have not signed it and is therefore illegitimate.

Given enforcement costs, prevention tends to occur more often, as a response to behavioral concerns, than increased penalties. The end result is growing intrusion in the private sphere and the proliferation of new regulations, new crimes without victims, and new bureaucracies to administer those intrusions.

The simplest cases involve preventing an individual's incarnation from harming another incarnation of the same individual.

▌ Protecting People against Themselves: Examples

In 2006 the French government, following recommendations from the World Health Organization and the European Union, banned *chocolate cigarettes*. Partisans of the ban argued that "research shows" that kids who were consuming chocolate cigarettes were more likely to be smokers as adults. The ban was opposed by others in the name of tradition and common sense. For example, historian Gilles Dal, in the French newspaper *Libération*, argued that it is stupid to allow both chocolate and cigarettes but not chocolate cigarettes; and that children are unlikely to think of them as a first step toward the "real thing." Most striking about this discussion, however, is that no mention is made of the role of parental authority nor of individual freedom. The arguments were purely instrumental: Is it doable? Is it logical? And will it indeed reduce smoking? Few commentators, if any, pointed out that some fundamental rights were at stake.

In a similar vein, many people advocate taxing unhealthy foods to fight phenomena such as obesity and heart diseases. This, for example, was proposed by my colleague Pierre Dubois in a 2007 article in *Le Monde*. He points out that the demand for "junk food" is highly price-elastic and therefore that a 5 percent increase in its price would reduce obesity by 15 percent. This falls clearly in the category of O'Donohue and Rabin's "sin taxes," discussed in the preceding chapter, and for this policy to be justified people must have the behavioral biases that prevent them from taking into account the effects of those foods on their weight. Notably he also shows that so-called junk food is the most intensive in calories for its price. Therefore junk food sounds like the ideal solution for the poor. The problem, however, is that the West's poor are no longer hungry; in fact, they eat too much!

These are examples of policies aimed at preventing people from indulging in addictive behavior on the grounds that they have multiple selves. There are also policies that regulate individual actions on the grounds that they are likely to be mistaken. Thus a French regulation, passed in 2004, makes it illegal for an owner to rent a dwelling if it is smaller than nine square meters. Because the tenant knows what he or she is renting, one may wonder why these transactions that should be mutually advantageous are banned. It is unlikely that living in a small room is addictive. So it must be that the tenant is "wrong" in signing such a contract, that is, that he does not properly evaluate his benefit.[2]

In a more complex version, paternalism imposes costs on one individual's incarnation to prevent another incarnation from inflicting harm on third parties. The logic is as follows: a person's "good" incarnation may voluntarily put him- or herself in a situation that makes it more likely that the "bad" incarnation will exert harmful actions. By banning or taxing the initial action we therefore reduce the frequency of the harmful action and somewhat increase the total level of "happiness" in society. The benefits are shared between potential victims and the "good" incarnations of individuals who are subject to behavioral biases, since these are spared the penalties associated with the deeds of their dark side.

This approach is clearly consequentialist: instead of considering the original individual as responsible and capable of self-control, instead we only consider the chain of events that may derive from his or her original choice and the total level of "good" that it generates. The approach is also statistical: the harm considered is neither certain nor likely; it is just that *on average* there will be less harm if a constraint is blindly imposed on all individuals.

The key point here is that rather than defining a clear frontier between a legal, harmless action, such as entering a railway station, and an illegal, harmful one, such as assaulting passengers, we now regulate the harmless action on the grounds that it may trigger an undesirable chain of events. Since most actions can sometimes have adverse consequences on third parties, the entire range of human choices is eligible for being constrained by the state. The reason for this evolution is that in a world of behavioral biases it is no longer obvious that the action, in the chain of events we consider, that directly and objectively causes the harm, can be treated as the result of a rational and conscious deliberation. Thus the trade-off between repression and prevention moves in favor of the latter, while at the same time concentrating all responsibility solely on the perpetrator of the harmful action becomes less morally defensible.

To illustrate that logic, consider an example inspired by the current politically correct atmosphere predominant on U.S. campuses. Suppose a male academic

---

[2] Needless to say, shortly after the law was passed, the media complained about a "crisis" in student housing.

economist has two incarnations: Dr. Jekyll, who abides by social rules, and Mr. Hyde, who tries to abuse young female students. Although only a few individuals have a Mr. Hyde sleeping inside their brain, and although he comes out very seldom, he nevertheless does so with some positive probability. Furthermore, and this is key, that probability depends on the circumstances. Mr. Hyde is more likely to come out if the male academic economist is alone with a female student in his office with the door shut, or in an elevator, or if he has been courting her for the last couple of weeks. It is natural, then, in order to protect the students against those instincts, to impose on the male academic economist actions that would reduce the frequency of such situations. That is presumably the role played by the now widespread social norm of leaving one's door open when talking with a student, as well as a host of "speech codes," sensitivity training, sexual harassment regulations, and the like. In short, although some kind of feminist bigotry can be blamed for these policies that are observed in many places, one can also attempt to ground them in a behavioral interpretation.

Note that, alternatively, one can also impose preventive measures on the potential victims (for example, instead of imposing an "open-door" policy, one could instead impose a modest dress code upon women). From a purely consequentialist perspective, this is as justified as putting constraints on the potential perpetrator. All that matters is which measure is most efficient on a cost-benefit basis. If the potential culprit's behavior is inelastic relative to that of the potential victim, it may well be efficient to impose constraints on the potential victim. This is clearly common practice whenever the potential culprit is irresponsible, as in the case of an animal.

As for the paternalistic policies already discussed, these have distributive consequences. They benefit the female students only if the gains from a lower probability of being abused outweigh the losses from the inconvenience imposed on them (for example, one does not necessarily want anybody to hear what's being said when discussing problems with one's thesis adviser, not to mention wearing a burkha). It is quite conceivable that the policies benefit the "Jekyll" self more than the potential victim, for example, by avoiding the costs of incarceration should a lawsuit follow from Mr. Hyde's behavior. And, again, preventive policies also harm rational people who do not have a behavioral problem.

Preventing Harm to Third Parties: Examples

An entire class of preventive policies that intrude on privacy concerns road safety. The alcohol content limits, for example, typically range between 0.02 percent and 0.05 percent. For an adult male weighing 160 pounds, this is at most two drinks. Thus such a policy is not so much about penalizing individuals for being drunk than imposing some "optimal" level of drinking on people, given how this affects their reflexes and perceptions. Privacy is ignored, and all that matters is the ultimate statistical effect on the number of accidents.[3] In many countries the use of cell phones while driving is also prohibited, and efforts are being made to extend that prohibition to "hands-free" devices; logically one should also ban listening to the radio or having conversations with passengers.

Gun-control laws are a similar example. Clearly they have little impact on criminals' ability to get weapons. Those who are restricted are the honest people who want to purchase a gun to defend themselves or practice a sport. Given that these people are aware that murder is illegal and know the associated penalties, and given that they are perfectly capable of acquiring the weapons they need should they decide to commit a murder or else do it by other means, it must be that the gun-control laws assume that people are incapable of self-control (although, again, most of the debate is instrumental, with partisans of gun control coming up with statistics and opponents arguing that the prospect that potential victims are armed deters crime).

Most Europeans would take gun-control laws for granted, but in the United States they are more controversial. The liberal English Bill of Rights of 1689 and its cousin, the U.S. Constitution, made self-defense a fundamental right and therefore insisted that citizens were allowed to carry weapons. Limitations were first introduced in Britain in the 1920s, and, in 1953, carrying weapons became illegal.[4] The magnitude of the restrictions imposed on British citizens in that area can be grasped from the following excerpt from a police website in the United Kingdom:[5]

> If you carry something to use for self defence, you run the risk of actually breaking the law yourself. Under the Prevention of Crime Act 1953, it is an offence to carry something made or adapted to be used to cause injury to someone. This includes things like a knife, bicycle chain or a sharpened comb.
>
> Under the Criminal Justice Act 1988 and the Offensive Weapons Act 1996, it is an offence to have anything with a blade or sharp point in a public place. Folded pocket knives are allowed as long as the blade is less than 3" long. Schools are specifically mentioned as places where articles with blades or points must not be carried, and the police now have the power to enter and search school premises if they have a good reason to believe that an offence of this kind has been committed.

Paradoxically self-defense is so vital that it has evolved into instincts, which is precisely a justification for paternalistic states to ban it, since such an instinct is equivalent to an incarnation that cannot make reliable commitments.

A surge has occurred in recent years in the discretionary use of so-called orders by which a court imposes restrictions on a specific individual so as to

---

[3] Ross (1984), in fact, argues otherwise, claiming that such laws are inefficient because it is practically impossible to increase the probability of being caught to reasonable levels.

[4] See Joyce Lee Malcolm 2003, at http://news.bbc.co.uk/1/hi/uk/2656875.stm.

[5] http://www.northants.police.uk/default.asp?action=article&ID=3224.

prevent further harm. Although the law defines which actions are illegal and which are legal, the order further defines a fraction of the legal acts to be illegal for a particular individual in a particular place during a particular length of time. Because the banned acts are themselves generally legal, the motivation is purely preventive. The British Anti-Social Behaviour Order (ASBO) was introduced in the 1998 Crime and Disorder Act. According to Wikipedia,[6]

> An anti-social behaviour order is an Order of the Court which tells an individual over 10 years old how they must not behave. An Order can contain only negative prohibitions. It cannot contain a positive obligation. In order to obtain an ASBO a two-stage test must be satisfied by the applicant authority (see s.1(1) Crime and Disorder Act 1998). The first is that the defendant has committed acts causing or likely to cause harassment, alarm or distress within six months of the date of issue of the summons. The second is that an order is necessary to protect persons from further anti-social behaviour.
>
> The applicant has to prove in a court of law that the individual has acted in an anti-social manner. The applicant must prove that the respondent has acted in such a manner beyond all reasonable doubt. *Further, each prohibited act must be an act preparatory to a criminal offence rather than the offence itself. In addition, each prohibition itself must be necessary. It would be inappropriate for a condition to be not to spray graffiti—the final act. It would be more appropriate for the order to prohibit the carrying of a paint-spray can in a particular area, marked on a map.* This would only be necessary if it could be proved beyond all reasonable doubt that the respondent continually created graffiti with spray-cans in a specific area.

The article then gives examples of how far this can go:[7]

- Two teenage boys from east Manchester are forbidden to wear one golf glove.
- A seventeen-year-old is forbidden to use the word "grass" as a term of abuse to threaten people.
- An eighteen-year-old male was banned from congregating with more than three youths, and he was subsequently arrested when he entered a popular youth club.

Similarly an article in the *Guardian* (2005) reports the following uses of ASBO:

> A twenty-three-year-old woman who repeatedly threw herself into the Avon was served with an Asbo banning her from jumping into rivers or

---

[6] http://en.wikipedia.org/wiki/Anti-social_behaviour_order#cite_note-napom-22.

[7] A great deal of confusion is added by the fact that a number of ASBOs actually ban illegal behavior. See, for example, the news item at http://news.bbc.co.uk/2/hi/uk_news/england/oxfordshire/5079204.stm. Thus there are two kinds of ASBOs: those that are redundant because they ban something that is already prohibited and those that infringe on basic human rights.

canals. A man with mental health problems was banned from sniffing petrol anywhere in Teesside. A woman living on an estate in East Kilbride was given an Asbo ordering her not to be seen wearing her underwear at her window or in her garden. The local Asbo unit handed out diaries to her neighbours to record when she was seen in her underwear, giving a new meaning to neighbourhood watch. All the people cited above face up to five years in prison for any breach of their Asbo.[8]

Preventive interventions penalize actions that are more difficult to observe and prove than usual violations of the law. Murder, assault, rape, and theft are associated with evidence such as bodies, DNA, window breaking, injuries, and so on. In contrast, it is much harder to prove that one has shown her underwear or has congregated with more than three people. In order to enforce such restrictions it is then natural to encourage people to report their fellow citizens to the government or to convict people on the basis of hearsay. Totalitarian states, which wanted to impose the same degree of control over private lives, although for different reasons, had to rely on similar instruments. Thus, according to the Wikipedia article,

> The fact that some of the evidence is hearsay without the possibility of cross-examination does not have the automatic result that the proceedings are unfair. The court will have to consider what weight to give to the hearsay evidence. The Court of Appeal has stated that the high standard of proof is difficult to meet if the entirety of the case, or the majority of it, is based upon hearsay evidence.
>
> Hearsay evidence is admissible by Civil Evidence Act 1995. Section 4(1) states that ... "in estimating the weight (if any) to be given to hearsay evidence in civil proceedings the court shall have regard to any circumstances from which any inference can reasonably be drawn as to the reliability or otherwise of the evidence."

A more extreme version of ASBO is SOPO, the Sexual Offences Prevention Order. It is well illustrated by a 2007 case, *Queen vs. Croydon Crown Court*.[9] The offense at stake would have been considered quite minor in most cultures for most of history:

> On 9th September 2005 he was convicted at the magistrates' court of an offence of sexual assault. What he had done was to sit next to a woman on a train. He had slid his hand along the back of the seat behind and underneath her, to touch her on the bottom from underneath, and that he had done twice.

---

[8] "A Triumph of Hearsay and Hysteria," *The Guardian*, April 5, 2005, http://www.guardian.co .uk/politics/2005/apr/05/ukcrime.prisonsandprobation.
[9] http://www.bailii.org/ew/cases/EWHC/Admin/2007/1792.html.

Nevertheless a SOPO was granted on the grounds that it was the fifth time the defendant was caught acting that way:

> Over that period of 30 years, the defendant had been convicted of very similar offences on a total of five occasions, including the most recent one to which I have already referred. The first had been in 1978. There had been two in 1986. There was another in 1995 and, finally, there had been the recent one in 2005. On all five occasions the defendant (as it is convenient to refer to him) had touched a woman on the bottom, on one occasion on the thigh and on one occasion in the groin area. They were all brief touchings done in public places, over the clothing. They were, however, touchings in very private areas and they no doubt caused a mixture of reactions which will undoubtedly have included anger, offence and in some cases anxiety.

The key justification for the SOPO was the defendant's alleged lack of self-control:

> In an interview with the police officer after the most recent conviction, the defendant had admitted that he sometimes got an urge to touch a woman and in effect he said that he did not on occasion resist it.

The SOPO's content basically amounted to preventing the defendant from using public transportation:

> The sexual offences prevention order which was sought was an order prohibiting the defendant from: (1) entering any railway station, save in the circumstances set out in paragraph 2; and (2) from travelling or attempting to travel by train or any public railway, save in an emergency or, alternatively, with the oral or written authorisation of the Metropolitan Police Public Protection Unit.

One may believe that this decision is extreme, since the physical damages are very small and no violence was exerted, while one imposes large restrictions on an individual's freedom of movement. However, this kind of utilitarian argument based on an objective measurement of damages can no longer be made if one adheres to the feelings-based ethics of post-utilitarianism. That is indeed the position of the court when it states that the touching caused anger, offense, and anxieties. These considerations allow the court to (artificially, from the traditional utilitarian viewpoint) inflate the damages in order to justify suppressing the defendant's freedom of movement.

Another instance of SOPO reported by the *Guardian* (2004) was issued against a man convicted of downloading child pornography:

> A former internet cafe worker, [...] is to be subject to Britain's first sexual offences prevention order (Sopo), which bans him from contacting or

befriending anyone under 16, or going within 100 metres of a school or play area.

[…] The wide-ranging Sopo, which lasts for a minimum of five years, will also prevent Fisher from living in or visiting the same house as a child, and from filming or photographing any child. He is also banned from using the internet to access pornography.

[…] The wide-ranging nature of the judge's order astonished civil liberties lawyers. Gareth Crossman, the head of policy at Liberty, said: "The breadth of this order is ridiculous. You cannot walk along a road without meeting a child or going within 100 metres of a school in most parts of Britain." He said it would give the police "utter discretion" over how it should be applied.[10]

Preventive intervention can also be noncoercive by influencing minds so as to reduce the probability of the harmful actions. There are two versions of such interventions. One is to promote a distorted reality in order to bias actions in the required directions (manipulating beliefs). The other is to train children to adopt the correct behavior. The former approach is clearly paternalistic, whereas the second is more arguable; a proper education may, in fact, improve freedom of choice if it teaches "noncognitive skills" that will help individuals overcome their own behavioral problems when they are adults.

▌ Distorting Beliefs and Preferences

Rather than imposing coercive restrictions, the paternalistic state may instead act directly on minds in order to reduce the frequency of the actions that it wants to deter. This can be done in several ways.

First, one may suppress information about some sinful opportunity so that people will not be tempted. This is the approach underlying a ban on advertising for cigarettes, alcohol, or gambling in, say, television. This type of ban is present in many countries. It is not clear whether the aim of such bans is to prevent the potential sinner from being aware of the product's existence, which artificially reduces his or her choice set, versus preventing the potential sinner from being artificially (and therefore inefficiently) teased into buying the product. In the first case the paternalist believes that if individuals knew what they can do, then people would make choices that eventually harm themselves. In the second case he believes that firms are exploiting the behavioral biases for profit, thus harming the individual's capacity for self-control (I elaborate upon this in chapter 11).

Second, the government itself may act as an advertiser and elicit emotions that would change the individual's preferences in a "desirable" way. The following piece of news illustrates such attempts, and how they may backfire.

[10] http://www.guardian.co.uk/society/2004/may/07/childrensservices.childprotection

OCEANSIDE, Calif.—On a Monday morning last month, highway pa-
trol officers visited 20 classrooms at El Camino High School to announce
some horrible news: Several students had been killed in car wrecks over
the weekend.

Classmates wept. Some became hysterical.

A few hours and many tears later, though, the pain turned to fury when
the teenagers learned that it was all a hoax—a scared-straight exercise
designed by school officials to dramatize the consequences of drinking
and driving.

Third, the government may promote inaccurate, false, or truncated information. One example is the denial by French officials that the Chernobyl cloud
had flown over France. It is consistent with manipulations aimed at suppressing
irrational reactions that would be costly. In that particular example, this would
have meant excess congestion and accidents created by panic-stricken people
attempting to exit the contaminated zone. A 2005 press release by Agence France-
Presse summarizes the controversy:

> French authorities deliberately suppressed information about the spread
> of radioactive fallout from the May 1986 Chernobyl disaster over France,
> according to details of an experts' report leaked Thursday. [...] The state-
> run Central Service for Protection against Radioactive Rays (SCPRI)
> knew of high levels of contamination in Corsica and southeastern France
> but kept the details under wraps. [...] The report states that the SCPRI
> issued imprecise maps that concealed the high levels of fallout in certain
> areas [...] It was the first time an independent study gave substance to
> long-standing accusations from anti-nuclear groups that the French gov-
> ernment deliberately played down the risk posed by the nuclear cloud. It
> also states that with full information health authorities could have taken
> targeted steps to reduce the exposure of vulnerable people such as chil-
> dren and pregnant mothers. [...] "There was a veritable campaign of lies
> instigated by the state in order to protect the image of the French nuclear
> industry," said the campaigning organisation Sortir du Nucleaire [...]
> "People should have been told not to eat fresh vegetables and milk prod-
> ucts" [...] However, scientific opinion remains deeply divided, with sev-
> eral renowned physicists sending an open letter to President Jacques Chi-
> rac in June commending [the SCPRI] for not giving way to panic in his
> handling of the crisis. [...] Doctors also question the supposed link be-
> tween Chernobyl and the rise in thyroid cancer, a trend which began in
> the mid-1970s.

This press release suggests that there is no compelling evidence that Chernobyl exposure increases thyroid cancer, yet the public and the "green" organizations seem to believe otherwise. Furthermore, the "green" organizations
certainly have at least as much media exposure as scientific studies. Absent

cognitive dissonance, the latter would be given far more weight by the public. Under cognitive dissonance, the repetition of environmentalist themes is likely to affect beliefs disproportionally. It is therefore difficult for the government to change those beliefs,[11] and it therefore faces a tough choice between a give-in strategy, which would have consisted in using the army and police to organize a costly, orderly, evacuation of millions of people, and a manipulative denial of the whole issue.

There are also, of course, many examples of less manipulative "awareness" policies. In many cases, however, their motivations are far more paternalistic than the goal of increasing the opportunities for people to solve their behavioral problems. In 2000, for instance, according to Cunningham (2002), the U.S. Congress, in response to a declining savings rate, imposed an "express educational mandate on the Department of Labor [DOL]."

> Its purpose was to advance the public's knowledge of savings and investment by requiring the DOL to gather and disseminate this knowledge, including by means of a permanent Web site and by requiring the President to hold periodic summits on the subject. [...] For example, it requires the teaching of compound interest and the virtue of early savings to take advantage of it. [...] the legislation compelled teaching the "importance" of "diversification" and "timing" in investing.

We see that even though the policy was noncoercive, it rests on the paternalistic assumptions that the U.S. personal savings rate is too low; that private markets cannot supply the right information to the people; and that the department of labor is the right institution for doing so. We will not comment on the irony that the government could well offset such deficiencies with its own policy tools but soon chose not to by having high public deficits and low interest rates.

The preceding discussion and examples illustrate the dual contradiction involved in moving from repression to prevention.

First, there is the logical issue that prevention can only occur at the cost of creating new criminal offenses for which a repressive infrastructure must be instated. This not only is a contradiction, but it is also a mechanism through which paternalism spreads *epidemically* to all areas of human behavior through a chain of preventive regulations, each one reducing the likelihood of a harmful consequence while introducing a new (generally victimless) harm. For example, once drunk driving is prohibited because people may create accidents, one may then prevent drinking because people might drive. And the chain stops when a whole block of human culture is eliminated, as was attempted during the prohibition era.

---

[11] This applies equally to an "objectivist" government that wants citizens to be as well informed as possible and to a paternalist government that wants to distort beliefs in its own way.

Second, the tension between prevention and repression is leading to an overhaul of our value system. Whereas some people end up in jail for socially constructed, victimless offenses or for minor offenses associated with very little harm, others are spared punishment on the grounds of their own irresponsibility. This is aggravated by the tendency of the legal profession to invoke "syndromes" in order to plead irresponsibility. In Pennsylvania, for example, in December 2007, a woman was cleared of having murdered her two children on the grounds that she might suffer from schizophrenia. Schizophrenia was not clearly established, but the presumption of irresponsibility prevailed even though the facts were undisputed. Furthermore, at stake was not so much an impulse but whether the person (or her relevant incarnation at the time of the crime) was "aware" that murder is illegal.

But an even more beautiful case (from the perspective of the argument made in this book) is the sentencing of a woman to just six years for having murdered her husband on the grounds that she was intoxicated with alcohol when perpetrating the act.[12] Thus a condition that transforms harmless actions into a crime, and can land a person in prison for years if he or she unwillingly causes an accident, can also substantially reduce the penalty if that person willingly commits murder. Indeed, the penalty imposed on this woman for a *voluntary* act is of the same order of magnitude as that imposed on drunk drivers for *involuntarily* causing lethal accidents.

Just like the mental states of a victim may transform an objectively harmless act into a criminal one, those of the perpetrator may turn objective harm into a therapeutic issue.

▮ Screening

A key dilemma faced by the paternalistic state is how to apply preventive measures. It must choose between two options. Either the preventive measure is applied uniformly, regardless of individual characteristics, which is typically what we observe for "mild" violations of individual freedom such as safety belts, limits on alcohol content in the blood, the use of mobile phones while driving, regulation of fire weapons, and so on. Or it applies to a subset of individuals on the grounds that their characteristics make them "likely" to cause harm, and this is typically the case for the SOPOs and ASBOs –style restrictions discussed above. The individuals in the latter case are screened on the basis of their record.

The intuitive appeal of such restrictive orders is that one is tempted to interpret them as a penalty imposed on the original illegal acts. After all, if one wants

---

[12] http://www.theaustralian.news.com.au/story/0,25197,24807655-2702,00.html

to avoid a SOPO, one may just avoid molesting people in public transportation. In my view, this is not a correct interpretation. Traditionally, an offender pays a penalty in the form of a fine or a jail term, after which one starts again with the same rights as other citizens. Thus there is no reason to use an order as a deterrent, since other deterrents already exist in the judicial system. The real motivation for orders such as SOPOs is that the record is used as evidence that the individual is "prone" to certain actions and the order aims at preventing the individual from putting himself in situations where he will undertake those actions. Essentially this means that it is equally legitimate to consider screening independently of the individual's record. In the above example, if prior to any wrongdoing some psychological test had revealed that the individual was predisposed to molesting women in public transportation, then it would have been justified to issue a SOPO against him, since the "social" costs and benefits of that SOPO are exactly the same as if the predisposition had been detected through the individual's action.

For a utilitarian there is no value to privacy. The only case against such screening is that it is useless if individuals are unitary and capable of self-control, because incentives through penalties then work.[13] Once individuals are assumed to be non-unitary, it is optimal to screen for predispositions and apply prevention selectively. In fact, screening makes it possible to increase the freedom of those whose test comes out "negative," thus reducing the implicit subsidy on irresponsible behavior. For example, one could lift alcohol content restrictions for moderate drinkers and impose them only on those who have been tested for a predisposition for heavy drinking. Indeed, some actual policies already have that element; when the legal drinking age was raised in the 1980s in the United States from eighteen to twenty-one, this was motivated by studies showing that eighteen- to twenty-one-year olds had the highest incidence of car accidents associated with DUI (driving under the influence). And in 1976 the state of Oklahoma, on similar grounds, set a higher drinking age for men than for women, since the latter are seldom involved in DUI-related car accidents. This was overturned, however, by the Supreme Court.[14]

This means, of course, the introduction of a caste society where people with different individual characteristics face different rules. Some will be prevented from taking public transportation, others from owning a mobile phone, and so on. But it is a mathematical fact (well known to providers of life or health insurance) that when seeking to maximize some objective function, one always does better by discriminating than by treating everybody equally. Discrimination increases the number of available instruments and is therefore superior to nondiscrimination. A policy maker who allows himself to discriminate may well eventually conclude that a nondiscriminating outcome is optimal, but that is a

[13] In fact, even that is true only in a relative sense; even if individuals are unitary one may want to do screening so as to tailor penalties to individual preferences. Nonunitary individuals then make screening even more valuable by allowing selective prevention.

[14] See Harsanyi 2007.

special case and is very unlikely; on the other hand, were he to restrict himself to nondiscriminatory policies, he would lose degrees of freedom and forfeit superior outcomes. This argument applies regardless of whether individuals are unitary; in fact, it holds whenever a social welfare function exists. It is ironic that modern Western societies are so concerned by discrimination in private transactions while adhering to policy views that typically refer to some social welfare function—implying that they should welcome discriminatory public policy.[15]

▌ Paternalism and Redistribution: Paternalism in the Welfare State

We have already discussed how a paternalistic perspective implies that redistribution should be conducted differently, by substituting ex-ante control and positive rights for ex-post conditional insurance. This is one aspect of the interaction between paternalism and the welfare state: the latter will be more intrusive, as is the case for other domains of government intervention, in a postutilitarian society. The interaction also goes in the other direction: the perceived value of paternalistic policies is itself greater, the greater the redistributive concerns. The underlying argument is that the poor are more likely to be behaviorally challenged, because such failures are a cause of poverty (if one cannot commit to waking up in the morning to go to work, he or she is more likely to end up on the dole). These views are well represented in a 2004 *Guardian* article by pro-paternalist journalist Jackie Ashley:

> This is a time of year and a moment in politics when the issue of ministerial lectures is particularly timely. [...] Hardly a day passes without new government-approved warnings on cholesterol, stress, sleep, sugar and exercise. New laws on using mobile phones while driving have come in. Ministers look on approvingly as the British Medical Association raises the question of whether there should be a general ban on smoking. There's been a "salt summit" on the use of coronary-threatening quantities of salt in processed foods. This is also a time of year when rocketing credit card debt has become a big public issue, and yet offers to borrow more money drop through the letterbox daily. As Britain's overweight, indebted families look blearily ahead into 2004, the government is on hand to teach them family values too. A raft of new measures aimed at the parents of anti-social children is now available to the police and courts. [...]
>
> It is time to stand up for the "nanny state" [...] And also, in general, for the state's right and duty to involve itself in questions of diet, health, family budgets and good parenting.
>
> [...] Affluent families have more freedom to deal with the consequences. They buy the fresh food which isn't loaded with sugar and salt. They buy

[15] Thus some economists openly advocate discriminatory policies; see, for example, Alesina and Ichino 2007 and the critique in Saint-Paul 2008.

mounds of expensive fruit for their children. They pay subscriptions for gyms and health clubs, and go on pricey diets. They are better educated about health issues and they buy the parenting books. They can respond to the latest "must-have" (always a lie) advertising for electronic goodies without falling into crippling debt. Oh yes, and they can buy in domestic help—nannies and their successors.

Who really thinks that a centre-left government should stand aside and do nothing? The whole point of progressive politics is to stand with the most vulnerable people. Today that means helping counter the great commercial, short-termist forces that rain down. [...] Today, in trying to help all families struggle with consequences of consumerism and social change, these ministers are doing a vital and noble job.[16]

Two ideas are evident in the preceding quote. First, behavioral issues like obesity and smoking are a problem of the poor, and therefore one should implement more paternalism, the more one cares about the poor. Paternalism is no longer only motivated by intrapersonal redistribution but also by interpersonal redistribution. Second, the causality between poverty and behavioral issues goes both ways, because behavioral issues can be solved by activities like acquiring education, going to the gym, and so forth, and the rich are in a better position to obtain these goods.[17] Thus commitment is no longer a matter of self-control, it is now supposed to involve resources and therefore is now regarded as a privilege.

To a traditional utilitarian, the question should be recast as follows: Why should we redistribute to the poor in any other way than a pure monetary transfer? Paternalists, in fact, argue in favor of a form of in-kind redistribution, which consists in helping the poor by controlling their behavior. As such, the view that commitment involves resources does not invalidate the standard economic argument that all redistribution should be in monetary form. After all, the poor can indeed use their transfers from the welfare state to purchase whatever commitment technologies they need. More serious is the other argument—that individuals who have commitment problems are precisely those who are likely to be poor. It means that they will spend the money given to them on the "wrong" goods. If they do, however, it means that this benefits at least one of their incarnations. To make a case for paternalism, we actually have to go back to intrapersonal redistribution and argue that another incarnation is harmed and that the social planner gives sufficient weight to that self.

---

[16] http://www.guardian.co.uk/society/2004/jan/01/futureforpublicservices.comment.

[17] The view that healthy food is more expensive, as the author suggests, is largely a myth. As far as proteins are concerned, many species of fish such as mackerel or sardines are inexpensive; the price of salmon and trout has fallen dramatically as a result of the ability to breed them. And if the obesity crusade is to be believed, people eat too much and could therefore substitute quality for quantity at constant total costs.

But that is not the end of the story, because the paternalist also has to explain why such restrictions should be imposed on everybody rather than only on the poor. The above-quoted article is silent on this issue presumably because the author does not value the welfare of the non-poor. But if we believe, as she does, that behavioral issues are essentially a matter concerning the poor, then it is unclear why all the paternalistic interventions that we observe also affect the rich. Why isn't paternalism just targeted to the poor, as it originally was with private charities and early welfare states? Even if the social planner is a pure Rawlsian who only cares for the poor, the rich would be happy, in principle, to pay higher taxes if as a counterpart they face less restrictive regulations; if this trade-off leaves them indifferent, the state will have more money to redistribute to the poor, who will then be strictly better off. So why should the rich who can buy diets, read books about cancer and obesity, and subscribe to a gym have to face the same distorted set of prices, and the same regulations, as the poor? One obvious answer is that it is difficult to discriminate between the two, because there would be some arbitrage going on between the rich and the poor that would prevent the targeted paternalism from working. Another might be that one wants to avoid the caste system envisaged above; but this is in contradiction with the rise of tailor-made preventive orders that we have discussed. If behavioral issues were mostly a concern for the poor, and if policy makers were careful about designing their interventions so as to minimize the harm to individual freedom, paternalistic interventions would be designed so as to be limited to the neediest groups. But this is not what we observe. Rather, redistribution is one additional argument used to justify the general trend toward more paternalism, which applies across the board.

Paternalism and Redistribution: Intrapersonal Redistribution

The case for paternalism on purely interpersonal redistributive grounds is therefore weak. How about intrapersonal redistribution? We have argued that, in theory, a post-utilitarian social welfare function could aggregate welfare across incarnations as if they were different individuals and even ignore the boundaries of the actual organisms in which those incarnations are seated. In practice, of course, it is far harder to establish that one incarnation is worse off than another incarnation of the same individual. In the utilitarian world, redistribution could easily be implemented in practice on the basis of revealed preferences: we at least knew that the poor would be better off with more money than with less. Now we do not even know that, and the literature on habituation suggests it might not even be true—thus redistribution could be questioned altogether, although I have not encountered any such doubt in the behavioral literature.[18] A

---

[18] This is presumably another manifestation of the "progressive" bias that has already been mentioned.

further difficulty with the intent to redistribute between incarnations of the same individual is that they share the same budget constraint; therefore the state cannot control how resources are allocated between incarnations. If that allocation were done efficiently, any attempt by the government to redistribute would be defeated by offsetting transfers between incarnations. Thus redistribution in monetary terms between incarnations is not feasible, since the government does not control which incarnation spends the money. Therefore we again expect more intrusive tools than redistribution to be used instead: direct restrictions on choices (strong paternalism), in-kind redistribution, and positive rights. This is indeed what we observe, but, to date, we lack a coherent framework that would define which incarnations should be considered as more deserving of public support. Thus policies that promote responsibility (or mimic it by imposing the responsible course of action) coexist with policies that reward irresponsible behavior. This contradiction stems from the fact that the neediest incarnation is likely to be the least responsible one, so that providing commitment and intrapersonal redistribution are conflicting objectives. Consider, for example, the policies that make it easier for drug addicts to access drugs (or substitutes like methadone), these policies are clearly a subsidy to drug use; the policy maker considers that easing the pain for these addicted individuals raises social welfare more than the reduction in social welfare associated with the greater incentives to consume drugs for nonaddicted incarnations. Yet, in other instances, we see policies, such as forced savings, that seem to favor the non-sinning incarnations.

This chapter has discussed just how wide-ranging government intervention can be once the liberal society is replaced by a post-utilitarian one. This raises the question of how this can be enforced. In the next chapter, I discuss how the attempt to efficiently enforce a broad set of constraints imposed on the individual is breeding further attacks on freedom and responsibility.

9

Responsibility Transfer

The examples discussed in the previous chapter illustrate how modern paternalism operates. For each individual action (e.g., taking the train), a chain of
potential consequences is derived, and if one of them is harmful (the individual
indulging in "improper touching"), then this justifies penalizing the action that
initiates this chain of consequences in addition to the penalties put upon the
illegal act at the end of the chain. The underlying logic is the mix between consequentialism and utilitarianism: all we care about is the average effect (in some
statistical sense) on our social welfare function of the individual taking the
train. If our computations, taking into account all effects through the chain of
consequences, shows that its value is reduced, then we prevent the individual
from taking the train.

Yet our examples and arguments, thus far, are "plagued" by remnants of individual responsibility. Although we do ban the individual from a harmless act
on the grounds that it would allow one of his incarnations to harm somebody,
these two incarnations are nevertheless located in the same individual. Implicit
in this is the assumption that incarnation A is liable for the deeds of incarnation
B because of that common feature. But if "we" are a pure post-utilitarian who
maximizes the total flow of happiness, and if we are serious in our behavioral
stance in treating A and B as two different selves, then there is no reason not to
extend paternalistic restrictions to the case where the incarnation at the start of
the chain of consequences is actually seated in a *different* individual from the
one who eventually perpetrates the final deed. This is the mere implication of
maximizing total happiness independently of its distribution across organisms,
that is, of aggregating the welfare of a collection of incarnations independently
of their hosts.

What Is Responsibility Transfer?

This leads to a new feature of paternalism: responsibility transfer. By responsibility transfer I mean holding an individual liable for a perfectly licit action, on

the grounds that this action has initiated a chain of events that has led to harm inflicted *by another individual.*

To clarify the discussion it is useful to emphasize what responsibility transfer, according to this definition, is not. Traditionally legal minors (children and, in the past, women) cannot be penalized for their actions, precisely because they are considered to be mentally incapable of responsibility. This usually results in a low penalty being imposed (as in the "syndrome" legal cases that now proliferate) or in a penalty being imposed on the parents on the grounds that they should exert proper authority. This is somewhat of a transfer of responsibility but it is not penalizing some action by the parent on consequentialist grounds. Instead, it is simply assuming that the parent has enough power—and society was traditionally enforcing parental authority, which is arguably no longer the case—to elicit the correct behavior in the child so that the parent can indeed be held responsible for the child's misbehavior.[1] Second, in some circumstances, people may have failed to take preventive actions that led to an accident; then, since the accident is not the outcome of anybody's will, if one wants to allocate responsibility in, say, determining damages, the whole chain of events has to be considered.

This is not what we are considering here, since we focus on an illegal or harmful action having been *chosen* by one of the people in the chain of events. But, again, it is notable that once individuals are treated as multiple and plagued by self-control problems, finding out which decisions have been made by whom in order to allocate responsibilities becomes less relevant. In particular, the difference between a chain of actions leading to an accident and a chain of actions leading to a crime is simply blurred.

Introducing responsibility transfer extends the epidemic spread of paternalism. Once we have ruled that the suspected sexual abuser (let's call him Joseph K.) is no longer allowed to take the train, we can impose restrictions on any individual who would incite him to do so. Thus we could sue Mr. A. for refusing to give him a ride or Mrs. B. for offering him an interview for a job far from his home. Virtually any event that affects the life of Joseph K. has a bearing on the extent to which he might want to take the train; therefore the only limit to the regulations we can impose on the individuals who interact with him is our own imagination.

[1] There are now many ways in which parental authority is no longer enforced by the state. In some countries parental punishment such as spanking is just illegal. Part of the underlying logic is, of course, that the parent is just another "behavioral" type who could merely be indulging in his or her violent instincts rather than applying a reasonable punishment. But then it follows that the parent should no longer be held responsible for the child's deeds. Quite naturally, then, we observe that "society" implicitly considers itself responsible, and inflicts upon itself some penalty such as increased spending on counseling, public dwelling rehabilitation, and so on, as a response to youth crime.

But it would be inefficient to apply responsibility transfer indiscriminately, since the individuals whom we restrict have their own behavioral problems, which raises the problem of designing an appropriate incentive scheme so as to manipulate the chain of events in the desired way. For example, a court could issue an "order" mandating Mr C. to give a lift to K. in his car every morning, which would clearly help to enforce the order preventing K. from taking the train. But if we suspect that C. is a compulsive drinker and might have an accident in which K. is injured, this is clearly a bad idea. If, instead, we suspect that Mr. D. is a responsible driver, it makes more sense to the social planner to impose the order on D. rather than C.

Thus the paternalistic society will naturally impose the burden of prevention selectively on the individuals who are likely to be rational and unitary. This is not for any redistributive reason but because it is the most efficient allocation of responsibility from a consequentialist perspective.

Responsibility transfer not only originates from the will to allocate responsibility to those who are rational; it is also determined by the relative capacity to pay of the various actors involved. This partly explains why there is a tendency to take into account not only the person's presumed cognitive capacity to act responsibly but also his financial capacity to pay the damages. In a world with limited liability, it is more efficient to allocate responsibilities to those individuals or entities that can pay: this allows one to increase the penalties and get better incentives. One can then think of "optimally" allocating liabilities to the actors in a chain of events by considering both their cognitive and financial capacities. This is indeed what the pure consequentialist would do. Actions are no longer considered independently and deemed good or bad, legal or illegal. Punishment is no longer applied to the perpetrator of the bad or illegal action. All that matters is the design of a global incentive system that maximizes aggregate happiness.

In some sense, responsibility transfer is a rediscovery of the virtues of decentralization which underlie the welfare theorems of the utilitarian society. A police state is quite costly, and rather than monitoring all the actions in the chain of events, the government can concentrate on action a as long as there is presumption that individual A is sufficiently rational to internalize the whole chain of events. In the extreme case, a caste society may evolve where some individuals are considered irresponsible and others are treated as super-responsible. Not only are they assumed to be capable of consistent rational behavior, but they are also supposed to internalize the behavioral problems of the others by computing the consequences of their own choices on the chain of events triggered by the other party's subsequent actions. Insofar as these consequences involve harm caused by people of the irrational kind, the rational originator of the chain of events is held liable. Society is now treated as a large extended family split between adults and legal minors, and the law differs between the two. Of course, the central moral hazard associated with this political system is that there is a race to be included in the legal minors category. Hence the proliferation of "syndromes" as exemplified by the case of a university professor who, under a charge of "sexual harassment," pleaded that he was mentally disabled—which means that the mentally disabled can be university professors, and, moreover, the codes pertaining to sexual conduct should not apply to them!

Then here is the central question: On the basis of what characteristics will the individuals bearing the burden of responsibility transfer be selected? We observe the following:

- Richer people are more likely to be held responsible based on the very practical matter, as pointed out above, that they have the ability to pay. Since responsibility is costly for the individual who bears it, a social planner is more likely to allocate responsibility to the rich, the greater the weight of the poor in the social welfare function—that is, the more the social planner is "Rawlsian." Furthermore, a sufficiently high income can also be used as the sign of an individual's capacity to act responsibly.

- People are more likely to be held responsible when acting in a professional capacity than in a private capacity. This is presumably because, in the first case, one is faced with an incarnation that is somewhat rational as it is performing a contractual task; in the second case, competition between incarnations is unleashed and behavioral issues are more likely to be important. Yet, as the examples below suggest, this is problematic to the extent that the restrictions imposed on an individual performing a job usually contradict his commercial objectives or contractual terms.

- Similarly moral entities like corporations are more liable than persons. By assumption, an organization is not subject to behavioral bias but is designed to maximize a well-defined objective, for example, profits. Thus it is efficient to transfer responsibilities to organizations, which is precisely what is achieved by the numerous regulations that are imposed on them regarding the health and safety, training, and information of employees. Of course, this view is incorrect from the very perspective of non-unitarianism. The organizations themselves are comprised of people, and if those individuals behave inconsistently they face sharp agency problems. Furthermore, the political economy critique applies there, too: any organization has internal conflicts of interests (think of divergences between shareholders, creditors, managers, and workers) and, for that reason, the organization as a whole need not behave consistently.[2] Thus responsibility transfer to organizations probably works poorly, but it is nevertheless commonly observed, perhaps again because of their capacity to pay.

Putting in place an "optimal" system of responsibility transfer is plagued by an ugly dilemma. Either one assigns people between the two castes on the basis

---

[2] One may recall numerous events of the last decade such as the Enron scandal, the excess risk exposure of banks in the financial crisis, and so forth.

of observable birth characteristics such as sex, race, or possessing certain genes. This would construct a new form of apartheid, albeit well intended; and one would have to rely on "science" to tell us how inherited genetic characteristics correlate with behavioral problems. Finally, the system neglects the individuals within each group who, for some reason, would not exhibit the corresponding behavioral traits. Or one relies on each individual's past record to build evidence of rationality, or lack thereof, and this gives incentives to individuals to act so as to appear irresponsible. In this case, obviously, the system ends up subsidizing the very outcomes it was meant to deter.

In both cases, it is in the interest of those who are responsible to discriminate against the irresponsible by refraining from interacting with them,[3] since this amounts to an implicit tax imposed on them should some wrongdoing arise as a consequence. The more they do so, the more society will be segregated between the responsible and the irresponsible. This then implies that responsibility transfer no longer works, unless another step in the infringement of freedom is taken by coercing the responsible individuals into interacting with the irresponsible ones.

Another dilemma is that the paternalistic state, in order to implement responsibility transfer, must take a stand on how proactive the responsible must be in monitoring the irresponsible. Should the boss of Joseph K., or his wife, physically block him from entering a railway station? Should Mr. C. be required to purchase a car so as to give the rides to Joseph K.? This applies to actions as well as information acquisition: Should Joseph K.'s boss install a microphone in K.'s office and record all his telephone conversations in order to detect any intent he might have to take the train?

Are we discussing a dystopian fiction, or does it resemble reality? The reader can judge by him- or herself on the basis of the following examples.

Examples of Responsibility Transfer

The Barman Cases

It is now commonplace in a number of countries to condemn those who supply alcoholic beverages to a person if, for example, that person causes an accident while drunk.

In 2002, in France, a man caused a lethal accident after having drunk the equivalent of eight glasses of wine at a bar. The barman was indicted and

---

[3] As an anecdote, this happened to me in 1995 when attempting to rent a house in the United States for me and my family. An owner of a house with a stairway refused to lease her property to me on the grounds that my three-year-old son might fall on the stairs; the fear clearly was that I could sue her for not having taken the appropriate preventive steps.

condemned as an "accomplice" to the accident. He was sentenced to two months in jail under certain conditions.[4]

The sentence states that it is the responsibility of persons whose business is to *sell* alcoholic beverages to *prevent* their clients, under certain circumstances, from *buying* such alcoholic beverages. The barman is not only forced to act as a policeman but is also required to do so against the objective interests of his business.

The sentence created a precedent, since French law states that one is prohibited from selling alcoholic beverages to people who are *manifestly* drunk. This was not the case in the example above; jurisprudence imposes upon the barman the burden of measuring a client's condition, but it does not provide guidelines that define what is licit and what is not, leaving the issue of proactivity entirely unsolved. Should the barman measure the alcohol content in his client's blood and stop serving beverages as soon as the legal limit for driving is reached? What if the client claims he is not going to drive upon leaving the bar?

In a related court battle in Ontario, the organizers of a private party were sued by the victims of an accident caused by a person who had attended the party. The Canada supreme court dismissed the case on the grounds that the organizer of the party was a private person and not a professional supplier of alcohol. This illustrates the point made above that corporations and people acting in a professional capacity are more likely to be subjected to responsibility transfer than people acting in a private capacity.

Similarly, in the United States, there is a trend toward compulsory beer keg registration. According to Harsanyi (2007), "the process goes like this: You head to the local beverage depot to purchase a keg for your barbecue. You're asked for identification. Then the store clerk, acting as a surrogate for the police, records your personal data, along with the keg's registration number for future use should any underage drinker be caught partaking from your keg's goodness in the future." Also, many U.S. states have laws similar to the French practice described above.

The Renault Moral Harassment Episode

In January 2008 the French automobile maker Renault was subject to an investigation from the French Department of Labor on a "moral harassment" case.[5] (A French law bans "moral harassment" in the workplace; it was motivated by the fear that management could harass their workers in order to make them quit rather than laying them off, which would allow management to bypass

---

[4] These conditions refer to the French system of "sursis" which means that the sentence will be executed only if the defendant gets some other conviction in the future. A description of the case is available at http://www.prochedevous-enligne.com/index.cgi?numero=91&type=article&pageid=461&archives=1.

[5] "Technocentre Renault: l'inspection du travail évoque un 'harcèlement moral,'" AFP, January 24, 2008, 00h04.

employment protection legislation.) A number of Renault executives who had been "overworked" committed suicide. Renault was *not* accused of imposing extra hours on these people; overtime work is tightly regulated in France, and a European labor standard precludes anybody from being asked to work more than forty-eight hours in any given week, including overtime. Thus there was no way that Renault could legally ask any employee to go beyond that limit. Instead, the harassment charge has to do with Renault failing to properly monitor its workers work hours in order to protect some workers from their *own* workaholic tendencies.

The question of the extent to which labor laws infringe on contractual freedom is an important one, but it is outside the scope of this book. The issue here is that Renault had no contractual or legal obligation to prevent its employees from putting in more effort than the norm. Not only is it not in Renault's interest to prevent its employees from working more than they are supposed to, but it is also difficult for Renault to become a "nanny" and tell its own workers to stop working. What prevents them, for example, from doing the extra work in their home?

This is a textbook case of requiring a corporation to undertake the monitoring activities of the paternalistic state.

The French Swimming Pool Regulation

A French law makes it compulsory for owners of private swimming pools to build a fence around it. This law has been motivated or at least buttressed by some well-publicized accidents involving small children. Note that it applies uniformly, regardless of whether one has children. Thus it is intended not only to protect the owners from their own presumed inability to watch after their own children, but it also makes them responsible for preventing *other* people's children from drowning in the swimming pool. The law is consistent with transferring responsibility for such accidents from the victim's parents to the owners of the swimming pool.[6]

Invalidation of Prenuptial Agreements

An interesting example of responsibility transfer involves the moral hazard problem of the welfare state. We have seen that a post-utilitarian is more reluctant than a utilitarian to condition welfare payments on past actions and will therefore be more tempted to use paternalistic preventive measures. Another possibility, however, is to shift the burden to other agents who are in a contractual relationship with the non-unitary individual. Thus Blomberg discusses cases

---

[6] Notably (but this may be a French idiosyncrasy rather than a general feature of paternalistic states) the government has not built fences along the numerous rivers and canals in the public domain along which scores of families with small children walk regularly.

of premarital agreements being invalidated on the grounds that enforcing them would put one of the parties in welfare dependency.[7] In such cases the court typically has set some alimony at a level larger than specified by the prenuptial agreement, so as to put the recipient above the threshold for welfare entitlement. Thus it is perfectly legal for an individual to put himself in welfare dependency by a lack of savings or not searching for a job but, should that be the outcome of a contract he voluntarily signed, this jurisprudence tells us that the other party is then held responsible for such dependency and is liable for a tax (in our example, the additional alimony) which represents the "external" effect of the contract on the public finances.

Freedom without responsibility for some and responsibility without freedom for the others paves the road to tyranny. Worse, once a system of responsibility transfer is in place, the implied mutual liabilities will ensure general political support for further government control. Although the bartender couldn't care less about what his clients do after visiting his establishment, now that he is held responsible for their actions he will be quite happy to support any coercive measure imposed on those clients, if such a measure reduces his own risk of being held liable. Indeed, his lack of control over his clients' behavior makes him a stronger supporter of the preventive policies than the clients' "good" incarnations would be; the "good" incarnation knows the extent to which it is capable of commitment and may not need the state's help, but the bartender doesn't know that and would rather err on the side of safety by supporting, say, a compulsory "ignition interlock device [that would] compel motorists to blow into a tube and pass an alcohol breath test before the car would start."[8]

---

[7] "Unconscionability: The Heart of the Uniform Premarital Agreement Act," available at http://www.sgcfamlaw.com/CM/Articles/Articles9.htm.

[8] Harsanyi 2007. Indeed, the device is already being made compulsory for the collective transport of children, and I am sure that generalizing its use to all drivers is just a matter of time.

10

The Role of Science

The organization of the liberal society is based on the welfare theorems discussed in chapter 5. Although these theorems are "scientific" in that their results are rigorously derived from explicit assumptions that are themselves cast in mathematical language, their nature is rather logical and philosophical. They are not scientific in the sense of the natural sciences; they do not attempt to uncover any law of human behavior that could provide guidelines on what exactly the government should do.

This is in sharp contrast to the paternalistic state. The paternalistic state needs precise information on the behavioral mechanisms underlying human actions; and, since it cannot rely on revealed preferences, it also needs to know the effects of those actions on happiness. Thus the paternalistic state must inevitably be grounded on a body of social (and psychological) research; social scientists are supposed to feed the policy maker with studies underpinning reforms in taxes, subsidies, and regulations meant to increase the overall level of happiness. In a nutshell, because the things people want are now distinct from what makes them happy, let us measure the latter directly and coerce people into wanting what they like.

Unlike the natural sciences, the social sciences are inevitably statistical. When documenting human behavior, for example, they can at most claim that this trait is present in a certain fraction of the population. A rocket builder knows that the laws of nature will apply to the rocket's trajectory no matter how it is built. Either the rocket flies or it fails to fly. But the social engineer of the paternalistic state must take into account that the "science of happiness" that is being implemented does not apply uniformly to all individuals. A policy that benefits some by preventing mistakes or removing their biases harms those who are immune to these issues. This difficulty, however, entirely disappears as long as the state is utilitarian or, more generally, pursues any objective that aggregates welfare between individuals, for the statistics are the only thing the utilitarian needs to know. Once the population distribution of the relevant effects and mechanisms is known, the social planner can safely use it to balance gains and losses across incarnations and perform the cost-benefit analysis of its policies.

There are countless examples of a public debate about a law that would strip people of their individual rights revolving around the existence or lack of academic studies showing that exercising that right has a statistical effect on undesirable outcomes. Here are a few examples:

- When Congressman Joseph Kennedy proposed a bill that would ban all advertising for hard liquors, it was defeated specifically because the Department of Health and Human Services concluded that "research has yet to document a strong relationship between alcohol advertising and alcohol consumption."
- Much of the discussion about violence on TV or pornography revolves around the issue of whether these are statistically linked to crime and abuse. Kendall (2007) summarizes the terms of the debate as follows: "A long-standing question in the social sciences concerns the relationship between exposure to sexually-explicit materials and various anti-social behaviors, among the most grave of which is the propensity to commit rape. *Understanding the nature of this relationship is clearly crucial to effective policy-making and judicial decision-making with respect to free speech and obscenity issues specifically, and to the regulation of private behavior more generally*" (my emphasis). Although Kendall's own study dismisses the view that pornography increases rape, why is understanding this link "crucial" to free speech and the "regulation of private behaviour"? This is because it is increasingly thought that free speech and privacy are not constitutionally protected fundamental rights but should instead be designed "optimally" by the government. Otherwise, statistical research on the effects of pornography, or any consenting interactions or contracts between individuals, could not possibly be "crucial" to policymaking.
- Since government restrictions on private economic contracts has long been more socially acceptable than the regulation of free speech, it is customary to evaluate economic freedom with respect to its effect on employment or GDP growth, independently of any principled perspective on whether that freedom is an individual right. Thus the French government recently contemplated deregulating shopping hours. Nobody argued that people should be free to open their shop when they wished. Instead, the decision hinged on how many jobs that would create or destroy, and the effects it would have on productivity and growth. This example illustrates the *measurability bias* of science: regardless of the issue of individual rights, some of the economic benefits of such a deregulation were associated with the greater convenience for customers, and this is clearly much more difficult to measure than productivity or employment. Precisely for this reason, these benefits were downplayed in the debate, which was therefore framed by the availability of instruments.

In all these cases the arguments are purely instrumental; the measurement of those statistical effects supersedes any legal or philosophical notion of what a legitimate government intervention is. And the debate is purely consequentialist in that there is no concern for the particular causal mechanism underlying those effects. Since the specific mechanism is morally neutral—that is, it is not taken into account in our paternalist's social welfare function—we do not care to know what it is, and indeed most of the studies do not attempt to identify it.

The point here is that, although the role played by social science is increasing, its content will be shaped by policy in a specific way, one that may be substantially different from the research directions scientists would spontaneously pursue if they were purely autonomous. Post-utilitarian society needs social science but not just any kind of social science: some research directions and methodologies are more likely to deliver quick policy advice than others. Under consequentialism, policy is more concerned with the effect of a variable on outcomes than with the mechanism through which that variable operates.

Returning to school curricula and happiness discussed in chapter 8, suppose a study shows that a given educational program reduces the incidence of depression. Knowing that is enough for the post-utilitarian to decide whether the program should be implemented, regardless of *why* it works. To a scientist, however, the latter question is the most relevant one. And, to a non-utilitarian who values freedom of choice, whether or not the program works by reducing freedom of choice or distorting beliefs about objective reality is relevant.

Science will also likely help to fine-tune discriminatory preventive policies by establishing how individual characteristics are correlated with behavioral traits, and by designing tests that predict a high incidence of those traits. At present, the forensic domain is at the forefront of such attempts. This is especially the case for sexual offenders, since nobody dares to advocate for their right to due process.

Thus a test called the penile plethysmograph is used to determine whether somebody is likely to commit sexual offenses in the future. The individual's penis is wrapped in a detector that measures its diameter, and the individual is presented with pornographic material. Often he is tested for a predisposition for child abuse, and the material he is shown is then illegal child pornography.[1]

---

[1] Notably, in many cases the crime committed by the individual is to have downloaded child pornography over the Internet. So here we have an example where law enforcers are committing a crime in order to prevent that very same crime. But, in fact, that comparison is misleading. The individual who has downloaded child pornography has not harmed nor constrained anybody, but the law enforcers who force the person to view pornographic material are clearly abusing him.

Why is downloading child pornography illegal? That is presumably because of the consequentialist argument that it increases the demand for child pornography and therefore increases the economic gains for the producers of such material as well as their engagement in the predatory pedophilic activities associated with the production process. Another issue, however, is why people advocate for the banning of *virtual* child pornography; that is probably a behavioral argument that virtual pornography would make it more likely that the individual would compulsively download real pornography even though his incarnation that downloads the virtual one is aware of the illegality of the real material.

The more the individual is aroused by the pictures, the wider his penis; this is then taken as a predictor of future sexual offenses. There is considerable debate about whether this method has any value at all in detecting sexual offenders, particularly given that it is just measuring an evolved trait (being aroused by nudity) presumably shared by most men.[2] This is yet another instance of the instrumental debates over the efficiency of policies, and that is not what we are interested in here. What is interesting about this example is that the individual is denied any capacity for self-control and free will and that his future voluntary actions are inferred from the measurement of a hard-wired unconscious process. In many cases, of course, the individual has been convicted of some form of abuse, so there is some presumption of behavioral issues. But neither being aroused by the test nor the existence of a previous offense implies that the individual is incapable of self-control. The liberal society dealt with this by increasing penalties for repeated offenses. This has the advantage of not restricting the individual's freedom once the penalty is completed while ensuring that those who are indeed incapable of self-control end up insulated from society for a very long time. The paternalistic science, however, does not really care about whether the individual is rational or not. What it cares about is the statistical correlation between the result of the test and the incidence of child abuse (and, indeed, most of the controversy around the use of the plethysmograph is about that number). If some day one designs a test that can show that an individual is capable of restricting his actions because of the penalties attached to them, the paternalistic scientist will be happy to use that test and let those who pass it go. At the same time he will advocate for preventing Joseph K. from using public transportation if he fails the test. Paternalists have no objections to not restricting rational individuals as long as "science" has proven that they are rational; that does not mean they value freedom but that it turns out to be efficient for some people to have a bit more of it, thanks to recent scientific progress.

As pointed out in chapter 8, there is no logical reason (other than costs) why such preventive tests should be limited to previous offenders rather than extended to the whole population (this is already the case for subjecting drivers to alcohol tests in many countries). At present the main obstacle is their unreliability; if such unreliability does not prevent their use in judicial trials despite all the provisions for due process, it is unlikely that any constitution would block the application of such methods to the whole population should policy makers be convinced that it may help improve "welfare."

▌ Science and Power: The Return of Discretion

A key aspect of science—especially social science—is that it is constantly evolving. In the new paternalistic societies, the limits of government intervention are

---

[2] See Simon and Schouten 1991; and Barker and Howell 1992

shaped by the state of knowledge in the social sciences rather than firm principles. Each freedom is conditional on science putting an approval stamp on it. The day it is "proven" that having that freedom statistically has harmful consequences, it may be revoked. If a new study uncovers a new phenomenon or invalidates previous findings on existing phenomena, the policies must be changed accordingly.

This is again different from the liberal approach of the Enlightenment which seeks to impose intemporal restrictions on the government through constitutions so as to limit its involvement in private matters. These restrictions were not grounded on a scientific claim that they had measurable positive effects; instead, they were based on philosophical (and untestable) claims about the inalienable nature of Man's natural rights.

Consequently, we expect paternalism to increasingly restrict the scope of constitutions in order to increase its margin of response to future findings about human behavior.[3] This weakening of constitutions has a number of key implications.

A first implication is that the scope for discretion in government policy has increased. Constitutions reaffirm essential human rights, but they also constrain the actions of future governments in a way that, in particular, prevents them from discretionarily reneging on their own commitments. The curtailing of individual freedoms on paternalistic grounds, as a by-product, widens the scope for such discretionary interventions. The American Founding Fathers were weary of such discretion, fearing it might restore tyranny. For this reason they made it a constitutional right to carry weapons, which allows people both to defend themselves and revolt against government abuse. But the paternalists believe that such a right statistically increases accidents and homicides. Furthermore (and this is a form of the framing bias which I discuss below), it is far easier to document such a link than the effect of gun control on government abuses, even though the cost of such abuses, when they degenerate into authoritarian governments, is far larger than the human cost of gun ownership. Through this example we see that the measurability bias runs against constitutions and in favor of discretion. By construction, constitutions are a safeguard against rare events, whereas science thrives on having a large number of observations.

Another example involves free speech. As discussed in chapter 8, there is a close connection between "speech codes" and the criminalization of "hate speech," on the one hand, and the post-utilitarian prevalence of feelings-based

---

[3] In *The Constitution of Liberty* (1960), Hayek already warned against how a purely utilitarian approach would lead to the abolition of constitutional rules: "The idea that each conflict, in law or in morals, should be so decided as would seem most expedient to somebody who could comprehend all the consequences of that decision involves the denial of the necessity of any rules. [...] few beliefs have been more destructive of the respect for the rules of law and of morals than the idea that a rule is binding only if the beneficial effect of observing it in the particular instance can be recognized."

ethics. Arguably many restrictions on free speech in Western countries are, in fact, unconstitutional, so we observe a failure to enforce the constitution rather than its replacement by a paternalistic one. Let us assume, however, that on some day the constitutions are brought in line with these new restrictions and that free speech provisions are lifted so as to let benevolent governments ban some type of speech if it is shown to be "harmful." Clearly governments will be tempted to opportunistically use such bans also to prevent expression of political opposition. Obviously we may envisage provisions that distinguish between that and "harmful" speech—we return to that later. But even if such provisions exist, the government may strategically use restrictions to bona fide "harmful" speech to buttress its own political goals. For example, anybody familiar with the British administration has seen signs that it is a crime to "harass" government officials; this makes it more difficult for people to defend their rights in case of abuse by the administration. In fact, losing one's temper and even resorting to insults when being subject to abuse is a natural reaction; such displays of anger are actually a biological signal of the protester's good faith. Repressing such reactions amounts to repressing the recognition that one has been treated unfairly, and if one does not repress them, one becomes an offender. In this example, awareness by the government of its employees' feelings is a strategic device to reduce opposition to its policies at the end-user level.

Let us put ourselves in the skin of a benevolent paternalist faced with these issues. We want to allow for the government to discretionarily intervene in individual choices if it is proven that such an intervention would have positive consequences for total happiness. But we also want to prevent abuses of power. How can we reconcile these two goals? Somehow we need a system of checks and balances that would let well-intended intrusions go through while blocking opportunistic ones.

A natural solution would be to create an independent body of social scientists whose approval (at, say, some qualified majority) would be needed for the policy to proceed. Clearly that would be associated with a host of issues: How would this committee be appointed? What kind of regulations must go to its clearing? and so forth. These particular issues are not my problem since I am not advocating paternalism here; however, this example illustrates that if one wants to provide foundations for increasing paternalistic state intervention while preventing government abuses, one must resort to giving even more legitimacy and power to the scientists. Here we have the second implication of the weakening of constitutions, namely, the buttressing of the power of the technocracy as a substitute for constitutionally imposed limits on government.

The rise of technocrats is not a new phenomenon, nor is the idea that society should be planned in a rigorous manner on scientific foundations, which goes back to at least Auguste Comte. In principle, a utilitarian government does not need elections. Once the social welfare function is agreed upon—and, though this problem has no satisfactory solution, any disagreement is in favor of some special interest—we can just delegate the implementation of the optimum to social scientists. In traditional utilitarian societies that are not concerned with what people want but how to give it to them efficiently, a central role would be ascribed to the economist. In a post-utilitarian society, which is concerned with the content of happiness, psychologists are likely to get more power, unless economists are clever enough to reform themselves and embody more psychology—that is, more positive statements about how people actually behave and feel—in their field, which is exactly what they are doing.

The more "science" makes progress, the more it becomes sophisticated and opaque. The eighteenth-century philosophers had a vision of a rational citizen who could achieve a satisfactory understanding of the consequences of many policy decisions by virtue of his culture and scientific literacy. In turn, that citizen was capable of judging whether or not that policy should be implemented, and this provided the foundation for democracy. Indeed, these philosophers were not keen on universal suffrage and restricted the franchise to people whom they thought had enough judgment (as proxied by wealth) to be able to participate in the decision process.

As specialization and complexity make progress, that view is no longer possible. The citizens must delegate knowledge to the experts, which in turn involves trusting them and thus abdicating one's critical mind. When contemplating a decision, the question is no longer whether people think it is good or bad (the assumption underlying democracy); rather, it is whether the experts have shown whether it is good or bad. Just as the progress of science reduces the scope for political choice, so does it reduce the scope for political debate. Indeed, one of the intellectual arguments for democracy, the Condorcet jury theorem, assumes that the purpose of elections is to elicit the true social value of a policy. If people observe that value with an error, and if these errors are uncorrelated across a large number of voters, majority rule will yield the best outcomes because the error components of many individuals will cancel one another. But this argument totally ignores the fact that some individuals may be far more competent than others, that is, they get a much smaller error. The theory then implies that they should be given more "weight." In the extreme case, a perfect "expert" who would observe the effects of the policy with a zero error should be given dictatorial power.

In other words, it is pointless for people who only disagree about the objective effects of a policy to vote on that policy. Instead, they should ask the most respectable panel of experts what they believe and then conform to their prescriptions. And this is more true, the more advanced and reliable the science: the eighteenth-century clubs of *honnêtes hommes* are accordingly deprived of their power, and that power is transferred to the positivist technocrat.

This statement is actually also true in a liberal society: one needs specialists to work out the effects of the policies. But although elections no longer have a role in revealing the course of action that is objectively best from the point of view of social welfare (conditional on social welfare being known), they still have a potential role in revealing the people's preferences. Of course, the policy maker needs that knowledge only to a limited extent, since, for excludable goods, the price system works well in allocating them consistently according to tastes. But for public goods and the correction of externalities it may be useful to ask people how much they are willing to pay for providing the former or correcting the latter. Thus, for example, a bill abating sulphur dioxide emissions at a cost to the tax payer will be accepted or repelled depending on whether the majority of the voters gain or lose from that trade-off. That is an imperfect mechanism, but at least there is a correlation between the result of the vote and the magnitude of the damage that the externality imposes on the people. Despite its dirigisme, technocracy draws a tight frontier between subjective preferences and feelings and the objective world of material objects. The "expert" is supposed to give advice on the implementation of the collective choices on the basis of his knowledge of the latter.

Unfortunately that frontier disappears when the technocrat becomes post-utilitarian. Science is then endowed with the task of measuring feelings and happiness and of measuring causal chains that transgress the frontier between the individual and the objective reality. A question that has not yet been asked is why those individuals should be expected to make the right choices when they are voting. Presumably asking such a question is a taboo, since a negative answer would amount to conferring dictatorial powers to the experts in computing the social optimum. Yet it is a logical implication of the post-utilitarian approach.

▌ The Political Manipulation of Knowledge

The more science becomes central in the design of policies and institutions, the more interest groups will try to take advantage of them to advance their respective agendas.

There is little vested interest in distorting the findings of hard sciences. People may benefit or lose from spending tax money for a space rocket, but nobody gains if such a rocket crashes. But when it comes to government intervention that is unrestricted by a constitution and typically creates losers and winners but is implemented on the grounds that a study has proven its positive impact on aggregate welfare (as opposed to being Pareto improving), it is clearly in the interests of the winners to produce such a study, and in the interests of the losers to produce studies reaching the opposite conclusion.

In the social sciences, one can merely vary sample periods, model specification, and estimation methods to produce a vast array of contradictory estimates, and then just cherry-pick the results one needs.[4] Some approaches are more

---

[4] A typical example is the effect of classroom size on student achievement. Hanushek (2002) has shown that out of 376 studies, 14 percent predict a significant positive effect, and another 14 percent predict a significant negative effect.

"robust" (less likely, say, to be polluted by bias) than others, but it takes substantial technical knowledge to understand those issues and such criteria will only eliminate a fraction of the available results. Another technique is "framing," whereby ideological bias is already embodied in the approach by picking a methodology which a priori rules out those findings and interpretations that would be inconsistent with the ideology. A government interested in justifying its own policies would simply allocate funding to research so as to indirectly perform framing and cherry-picking. The involved researchers may be perfectly sincere, and extremely competent: it is enough to truncate alternative approaches by cutting their funding to achieve the desired result.

Above we have mentioned how complexity and opacity progress in line with science. This reduces the number of interested parties who can critically assess its findings and opens the scope for manipulation by a small number of people. Whereas hard sciences rely on replicable controlled experiments, social sciences rely on correlations that are not necessarily causal and are difficult to interpret. This opens another avenue for political manipulation by advertising findings whose limits are poorly understood.

But the most striking aspect is that post-utilitarianism provides its own foundations for manipulating scientific knowledge. Because individuals are plagued by behavioral biases and cognitive dissonance, it makes sense to manipulate their beliefs, and examples of such manipulations have been provided in chapter 8. Since the dissemination and presentation of scientific findings themselves affect beliefs, we should not be surprised to see paternalistic attempts to distort those findings. The work by Salanié and Treich, discussed in chapter 7, suggests that one motivation for such distortions could be taking into account the public's irrational reactions to the findings. Indeed, we could even expect some policy-conscious scientists to misreport their own findings in order to convey the beliefs that would trigger the best reaction from the point of view of their conception of social welfare. Arguably, such attitudes have been elicited and questioned in recent controversies over climate change.

Depending on the issue at stake this may lead to overstatement or understatement. Typically, overstating the damages caused by addictions like smoking will have the same effects as a tax on smoking and benefit long-run selves while deterring short-run ones from smoking. On the other hand, understatement is expected to prevail when it is feared that the public would overreact to the findings. Manipulation, then, is a saving device that allows governments to avoid implementing the costly preventive measures that are needed to avoid panic. Manipulation can be light (the way the results are presented) or heavy (cutting funding on, say, the risks of nuclear plants).

Now it is easy to dismiss these concerns as Orwellian fiction and to trust the scientists' integrity and career concerns. But, in fact, scientists are subjected to the same biases as other humans and are likely to engage in framing and cherry-picking to push the conclusions that they like; additionally, funding may use career concerns as a tool to direct research toward predetermined conclusions. In chapter 8 we already have seen how an official scientific body can engage in misreporting. In *Nanny State* (2007), David Harsanyi gives some examples of paternalistic biases in scientific studies. In 2004, for example, the Center for Disease Control and Prevention (CDC) released a study which revealed that "overeating was responsible for an extraordinary death toll: 400,000 Americans in 2000—a 33 percent jump from 1990." However, the subsequent debate revealed that the study was flawed in a systematic way: "The first salvo came in 2004, in the pages of *Science* magazine. The investigative piece claimed that some researchers, including a few at the CDC itself, dismissed the report's prediction, maintaining that the underlying data were quite unconvincing." Harsanyi then describes how dissenters within the CDC censored themselves, partly out of career concerns. Then, in November 2004, the *Wall Street Journal* reported that the study had "inflated the impact of obesity on the annual death toll by tens of thousands due to statistical errors. [...] But that didn't stop many nannies from brandishing the dubious numbers until the CDC was finally forced to disclose their gross miscalculation. With a different team of CDC scientists and more recent data, they revised their numbers to 112,000 deaths a year. In April 2005 The *Journal of the American Medical Association* [...] concluded that obesity was responsible for around 25,000 American deaths each year."[5]

This example shows that the distinction between the bureaucracy, which would manipulate scientific knowledge to distort beliefs in the name of the common good, and interest groups, which would do so to advance their own agenda, is somewhat artificial. In the end, bureaucracy is split into a number of agencies that have some degree of autonomy and pursue specific self-serving goals rather than the maximization of some social welfare function. An agency like the CDC is likely to get a bigger budget if it can convince the public that there is some relevant crisis on which something should be done. This means that rather than acting as a benevolent paternalist who tries to lie to the people "optimally" so as to elicit the desired response, it will act like an interest group and push its own agenda unconditionally. Hence the Environmental Protection Agency (EPA) released a study in 1992 which claimed that secondhand smoke caused three thousand cancers each year. This study was invalidated by a court in 1998 on the grounds that the EPA had acted in "complete disregard of statutory procedure. In addition, they had cherry-picked data, evaded review by outside experts, and altered the methodology during the course of study."[6]

---

[5] Attempts to distort the dissemination of scientific findings can also originate in special interest groups rather than a paternalistic government. An illustration is the controversy that occurred in France in 2000. Unions at the statistical administration protested the publication in its journal of an econometric study by two leading economists, Guy Laroque and Bernard Salanié (2002), which showed that the French minimum wage destroyed jobs. They insisted that alternative studies existed pointing to an opposite conclusion and pressured the management of that administration to state publicly that it did not endorse that study. Although the episode is not related to paternalism, it illustrates the high stakes of social science today and the union's belief that such a study is a political weapon that may weigh in favor of political reforms that they expect would harm them.

[6] Harsanyi 2007.

I am not advocating that scientific evidence should be disregarded in the decision-making process. That is obviously a recipe for poor outcomes. Instead, I am pointing out that the increased power and reliability of Science makes it all the more important that strict limits define what is an acceptable government intervention and that it is socially accepted that policies which trespass those limits cannot be implemented regardless of their alleged beneficial outcomes. We are going in the opposite direction from such discipline.

11

Markets in a Paternalistic World

So far we have discussed how post-utilitarianism attempts to regulate individual actions and interactions with others. We now discuss how it is affecting the more impersonal and large-scale interactions that take place in markets.

Rationality and Market Efficiency

In a market we expect supply and demand to be equalized because prices adjust until that equilibrium point is reached. If there is oversupply initially, we think prices will fall. If there is an excess demand, they will rise. And we believe that the point where supply equals demand is the efficient one, because at that time the price reflects *both* the true cost of producing the good and the true value of the services the good brings to the consumers. All producers who participate in the market make a profit, or else they would not produce—hence their (marginal) cost of production is lower than the price. All buyers get a utility which, in monetary terms, exceeds that price; otherwise they would not buy the product. Hence all the goods sold give a greater utility to the buyer than what it cost to the seller. Furthermore, any producer who does not participate in the market does so because his cost is higher than the price, or the consumer does so because he would get less from the product than what it costs. Thus all the transactions that *do not* take place would be inefficient if they did. But if the price were, say, too low, then one of two things should happen. Either some producers are forced to meet demand even though their cost is larger than the price, implying that it may be larger than their additional customers' willingness to pay for the good. This forces some inefficient transactions to take place. Or some customers are not served, despite the fact that they are willing to pay more than the price, and therefore also potentially more than the cost of some idle producer. The result is that some efficient transactions do not take place. This is why the equilibrium price that equates supply and demand is also the efficient one in that it delivers the highest possible total surplus.

The problem is this: by what mechanism do we expect the economic agents to coordinate on the equilibrium price? This complex question is, in fact, unresolved, because it must hinge on a theory of how producers set prices when the market is not in equilibrium. But any such mechanism greatly depends on the assumption that individuals are rational. Suppose that the price is initially too low and customers are rationed. Some producer whose cost is higher than the price (call it an "entrant") may decide to attract some of the consumers who are not served by charging a price higher than its cost. The fraction of rationed consumers whose willingness to pay is higher than that new price will buy the good from the producer. This generates some mutually profitable transactions that would not have taken place in the original situation. And this would have been impossible if the initial market price were the equilibrium price, because in equilibrium all consumers willing to pay the price are served, and that, of course, includes those who are willing to pay more than the entrant's production cost. Most important, the entrant's behavior tends to bid the market price up, thus pushing the economy toward equilibrium. In other words, adjustment toward the equilibrium price is the agents' rational response to the disequilibrium. Similarly, if the price were too high, some suppliers who cannot sell their product would increase their profit by lowering their price and attracting consumers.

All this means that the efficient functioning of markets largely depends on the rationality of participants. Reaching equilibrium depends on arbitraging on both sides of the market. Consumers must realize that they are better off replacing their supplier with a cheaper one or paying a higher price at one outlet rather than being rationed at another, cheaper outlet. Similar rational decisions have to be made on the supply side.

If one questions the assumption of individual rationality, then one is led to doubt the capacity of markets to clear competitively and efficiently. Consider some of the behavioral biases we have discussed. Loss aversion, for example, may induce consumers to stick to a low-price supplier instead of switching to a high-price one, despite the fact that they are rationed and have a small probability of being served. This hinders the mechanism of upward price adjustment that is necessary to restore equilibrium when demand exceeds supply. Cognitive dissonance may lead people to believe that their regular supplier offers some exceptional service, or that he is particularly cheap, implying that they will have low incentives to collect information about the prices of other suppliers and to switch to the cheaper ones. Hyperbolic discounting may induce people to procrastinate in making switching decisions, to the extent that such decisions have a cost. Indeed, a literature on "customer markets" deals with the role of costs in changing suppliers.[1] Behavioral biases are likely to increase those switching costs, thus reducing competition and efficiency.

If markets clear efficiently, we expect the "law of one price" to hold. This simply means that all the producers of a given, homogeneous, well-defined product charge the same price. Otherwise, customers would pick the cheapest

---

[1] See Stiglitz 1984; and Phelps 1994.

producers, and this would either drive the price of those suppliers up or drive the more expensive producers out of the market; the process would continue until the law of one price holds. Empirically, however, the law of one price is often rejected by the data.[2] Thus Lamont and Thaler (2003) document substantial heterogeneity in the pricing of fairly homogeneous financial products. Lee and Malmendier (2007) show that in eBay auctions where buyers have the option of purchasing the same product at a fixed price in a non-auction eBay offer, the final price of the auction exceeds the fixed price in 42 percent of cases. It is hard not to ascribe such an outcome to behavioral biases.

Rationality is also needed on the supply side for markets to operate efficiently. Managers must make the right investment decisions, namely, those which maximize the value of the firm. Not only must the firm design an appropriate incentive scheme to induce the manager to maximize shareholder value rather than extracting private benefits such as corporate jets, it must also make sure that the manager responds rationally to those incentives. Yet a growing literature documents the behavioral biases of managers. Hence Malmendier and Tate (2005) find evidence of overconfidence for a substantial fraction of the top five hundred managers (from 20 percent to 80 percent of the managers suffer from overconfidence, depending on which measure is selected). For example, they would typically purchase shares of the company in excess of their stock options even though these options already overexpose them to their company's idiosyncratic risk. The authors show that overconfidence leads managers who disagree with the market to use retained earnings to finance projects that the market would not have financed. This leads to an inefficient portfolio of projects as well as an excess sensitivity of investment to the firm's cash flow.

How does behavioral bias affect markets as a whole? Odean (1998) analyzes theoretically how a financial market behaves when all participants are overconfident. He argues that overconfidence increases trading volume and price volatility. Notably overconfidence does not necessarily reduce the efficiency of the market if some traders are better informed than others. Thus, if there is some market failure, adding a behavioral bias does not necessarily make things worse.[3]

Also, individual inefficiencies on the supply side are less damaging to markets than when they come from consumers. If individual savers maximize their rate of return, and if consumers select the firms with the lowest prices, resources will eventually be allocated to the most efficient organizations. Going back to the overconfidence argument, if some nonbiased managers generated greater returns, then firms that employ them would finance themselves more easily and

[2] A large empirical literature studies the law of one price for homogeneous goods across countries, but that is less relevant to our discussion. See, for example, Haskell and Wolff 2001.
[3] There is a general negative result in economics that if the initial situation has some market failure, "anything can happen": opening an extra market can be harmful, adding a distortion can increase welfare, and so can a government policy despite the fact that it intervenes in an area unrelated to the original market failure.

charge lower prices to customers, since their wiser projects enhance their productivity. So we expect arbitrage in goods and financial markets to deliver the best allocation of managers. It is quite possible that a large fraction of the Fortune 500 managers are indeed overconfident; however, if this is associated with, say, better motivation and creativity, these managers are nevertheless those who are best from the viewpoint of shareholder value among a pool of heterogeneous potential managers who differ in many of their characteristics.[4] Selection is ultimately exerted by savers and customers, namely, individuals, and if they are rational they will select the most efficient organizations among a set of feasible outcomes:[5] maybe the perfect manager who maximizes the value of the firm would do better, but such a manager does not exist.

If one assumes, however, that investors and consumers are incapable of arbitrage because of their own behavioral biases, then this selection mechanism is shut down and the producers' biases now have an impact on outcomes.

The reader will not be surprised, at this stage of the book, that behavioral economics is then naturally used as a justification for greater government regulation of markets, since we no longer expect individuals to select the most efficient goods, strategies, and organizations. To quote Choi and Pritchard (2003):

> Adherents to behavioral law and economics are not so sanguine about investors' capacity to fend for themselves. They argue that arbitrage will not drive irrationality from the market but instead may fuel it: "Arbitrage is a double-edged blade: Just as rational investors arbitrage away inefficient pricing, foolish traders arbitrage away efficient pricing." If mispricing is a persistent phenomenon, the behavioralists fear that investors left to the mercies of unscrupulous brokers and corporate executives will be systematically fleeced. [...] Several commentators use the evidence of cognitive defects among investors to justify preserving and expanding the role of the SEC [Securities and Exchange Commission]. In the absence of government regulation, greedy promoters will step into the void to prey on the cognitive defects of investors. Particular scorn is directed toward proposals to substitute market regulation for SEC oversight. Market participants, the argument goes, will not precommit to regulatory protections to win the trust of investors but will instead manipulate investors' biases systematically to enrich themselves. Competition cannot be relied upon to promote investor welfare because of the systematic nature of the biases. The small investor cannot count on the smart money to demand fair treatment for all investors—the smart money suffers from the same set of biases. Only government intervention can protect investors from their own cognitive defects.

---

[4] This view is validated by Bertrand and Shoar (2003), who find a substantial effect of manager fixed effect—that is, a variable capturing the manager's own "style"—on firm performance.

[5] For an analysis, see Saint-Paul 2007.

The difficulties start when one realizes that many cognitive biases have been documented and that there is no clear basis to gauge their relative quantitative importance; for example, whereas the "availability bias" implies that markets would overreact to news, cognitive dissonance—confirmatory biases—have the opposite implication. These difficulties do not prevent some authors from proposing corrective regulations for the biases of market participants. It is already the case that brokers and financial intermediaries are required to review information about their clients' income, tax status, and investment objectives. Cunningham (2002) proposes to extend that and to force brokers to monitor their clients' psychological profiles, document potential biases and inconsistencies, and adjust their investment proposals accordingly:

> It would not be hard in such a meeting, or on the account form, to call attention to aspects of investor psychology in addition to investor financial condition. An applicant would check boxes according to investment objectives and also according to psychological profile. As with investment objectives, firms could choose which of various psychological factors seem most relevant to their understanding of what investments would be suitable for a particular client. [...] These profiles would then be considered in relation to otherwise stated investment objectives. In some cases the two may have to be reconciled according to some trade-offs. For example, an investor checking "speculation" as her objective and also indicating a steep gain:loss value function would clearly need to reconsider at least one of her choices. This could be done by the client at the outset or could be amended in the course of investment selection. In any event, the suitability of investment would be measured in terms of both financial objectives and psychological profile.

What is recommended here is simply that the broker (presumably a highly paid person) acts as a nanny. The author is silent, however, about who is supposed to monitor the (supposedly behaviorally challenged) broker and how liable he should be for his client's own mistake, that is, how much responsibility should be transferred to the broker. It is not logical, in particular, to implement a law based on the assumption that the investor is incapable of responsible choice while not transferring responsibility.

The author then considers, without reaching a definite conclusion, whether one should regulate equity issues to prevent firms from taking advantage of overvaluation. This would amount to considering cases where the firm "knows" that its share is overvalued because of irrational market participants as similar to cases of insider trading where the firm does not disclose relevant information that would reduce its stock value. Should such regulation be implemented— and there would be considerable practical difficulties in defining just what an overvalued stock is—it would be a clear case of responsibility transfer where the supplier of the stocks, in the same fashion as the barman, is held responsible for its clients' addiction to its product. And it again runs against the suppliers' profit maximization objective. But suppose that the firm needs to recapitalize itself (for "fundamental" reasons) at a time when its stock is overvalued; what is it supposed to do? One possibility is to sell it at the lower, "fundamental" price—it is unclear, however, how the price should be determined and the firm has an interest in imputing the highest possible one;[6] another possibility is to disclose its belief that its own stock is overvalued, as did Warren Buffet in 1996.[7] However, one does not see why "behavioral" markets should react rationally to such strange announcements, which may well trigger a selling panic.

To conclude: proposals have been made to extend existing financial regulations in order to correct behavioral biases so as to replicate, or converge to, market efficiency. This is a daunting task both because the response to such regulations will be "behavioral" in a way that is difficult to predict and because all market participants have biases, including the regulators themselves, as Choi and Pritchard (2003) pointed out. From our point of view, these attempts are essentially a nail in the coffin of individual responsibility.

▌ Markets as a Catalyst for Sins and Mistakes

For the paternalists, markets are suspect not only because biases fail to deliver the proper amount of arbitrage. They are also unlikely to yield the right mix of goods.

In the liberal society, the legitimacy of private contracting comes from the assumption that both parties are rational and act in their own interest. Such legitimacy is therefore gone in the post-utilitarian society.

In chapter 7 we have discussed how, if people make mistakes, government-imposed restrictions may increase total welfare. Let us use a simple example to illustrate how such restrictions may consist in interfering with the functioning of markets.[8]

An economy can import coconuts, at a cost equal to 10. Some people like it, meaning that a coconut brings them more happiness than its cost. Now assume that happiness can be measured in monetary units and people get 12 units of happiness out of a coconut. Their net increase in happiness is therefore equal to $12 - 10 = 2$. Other people like coconuts less and get only 5 units of happiness out of a coconut. If they purchase a coconut, their net welfare falls by $10 - 5 = 5$ units. As a shortcut, let us say that they do not like coconuts, but, in fact, they

---

[6] Because its customers initially believe that the correct price is the inflated one, it should not be difficult for the firm to place its new issue as long as the new price is below the initial one.

[7] When issuing shares for his company, Buffett ran the following advertisement: "Mr. Buffett and Mr. Munger believe that *Berkshire's Class A Common Stock is not undervalued at the market price stated above. Neither Mr. Buffett nor Mr. Munger would currently buy Berkshire shares at that price, nor would they recommend that their families or friends do so.*" Cited in Cunningham 2002.

[8] The following discussion is based on Saint-Paul 2002.

like them less than what it costs. Let us now assume that each group comprises 50 percent of the population.

If nobody makes mistakes, then only the group who likes coconuts will buy them. "Social welfare" is then necessarily improved when the market for coconuts is open. If, say, there are one million people in the country, and if I add the welfare gained by all the people who buy a coconut, then social welfare increases by $500,000 \times (12 - 10) = 1,000,000$ units as a result of opening the market for coconuts. Suppose now that people make mistakes in evaluating their own taste for coconuts. Assume 20 percent of those who like coconuts think they don't like them, and the same for those who do not like them. There are still 500,000 people who buy coconuts, but 100,000 of them do so despite not liking them (furthermore, another 100,000 abstain from buying them even though they like them). The effect of the market for coconuts on social welfare is now $400,000 \times 2 - 100,000 \times 5 = 300,000$. Thus it is much lower. Now if 40 percent of the people make mistakes, 200,000 people out of 500,000 will buy coconuts while not liking them, and social welfare is now $300,000 \times 2 - 200,000 \times 5 = -400\,000$.

Suppose the government's statisticians, who cannot precisely identify who likes or dislikes coconuts, nevertheless know their proportion in the population as well as the proportion of people who make mistakes. They then can compute total welfare as we did, and, using the last example, they would recommend shutting down the market for coconuts whose contribution is negative. The market is not operating well because too many people make the wrong decision. Note that the decision is not neutral from a distributive viewpoint. The unmistaken consumers lose, whereas the others gain from being prevented from making their mistake. This example provides a utilitarian rationalization for policies such as the banning of small room rentals in France.

Twisting that example a bit gives us another insight. Suppose now that coconuts come in two types: high quality and low quality. Assume that the low-quality coconuts only cost 8 instead of 10, and yield 9 units of welfare to those who like coconuts and only 2 units to those who don't. Suppose that everybody is presented with the opportunity to buy exactly one coconut and that this coconut may be of high or low quality depending on the circumstances. We see that the welfare gain to buying a low-quality coconut is now $9 - 8 = 1$ for those who like them and $2 - 8 = -6$ for those who don't. Assume that 500,000 people are presented with a high-quality coconut and the remaining 500,000 with a low-quality coconut. Then, under a 20 percent mistake rate, 250,000 people will buy a low-quality coconut, and 50,000 of them, in fact, don't like coconuts. Thus the contribution to the total welfare of the low-quality coconuts is $200,000 \times 1 - 50,000 \times 6 = -100\,000$. On the other hand, the high-quality coconuts positively contribute to the total welfare by an amount equal to $200,000 \times 2 - 50,000 \times 5 = 150,000$.

A paternalistic policy would now consist of shutting down the market for low-quality coconuts. But it may be that the characteristics of a coconut are not observable to government statisticians. In such a case, the government may nevertheless reach its goal by imposing a price floor on coconuts at least equal to 9.5. At such a price nobody wants to buy the low-quality coconuts. This shuts down that market but maintains the market for the high-quality coconuts. People who make no mistake and are presented with a low-quality coconut lose, but those who make mistakes gain, and the government, adding the welfare of all people, considers that there is a net total gain.

Here we see how paternalistic governments can intervene in markets by imposing price restrictions on transactions. Such restrictions "work" because prices are a statistical signal that may be used by the government to infer the likelihood that a mistake has been made as well as the size of that mistake. By regulating prices, the government is thus screening transactions in such a way that those that go through are, on average, less plagued by mistakes. Such interventions again run counter to the liberal view that people should be responsible for their own choices, but they are welfare-improving from a utilitarian viewpoint.

In those examples, policy interventions are preventive. But one can equally argue that private contracts can be invalidated ex-post. This could be justified both on the grounds that the contract resulted from a mistake and on the grounds that it was signed by a different incarnation. Clearly this can be exploited by a party in an attempt to renege on its contractual obligations. One may fear that the progress of paternalism jeopardizes the whole system of private contracting.

Another reason why the paternalistic policy maker is suspicious of markets is that they will inefficiently exploit behavioral biases for profit. For example, drug dealers or marketers of other addictive products will have an interest in giving away their product for free in order to stimulate the addiction. Advertisers may manipulate the context to convince consumers to buy the product. This includes many common examples. Instead of quoting a price of 10, the advertiser may quote 15 and pretend that there is a 33 percent discount: the higher price serves as a reference point compared to which the consumer believes that he is making a gain. Endowment effects are regularly exploited by offering free trials. Mental budgeting is used by offering "free" gifts should the order exceed some level. Firms also take advantage of hyperbolic discounting to offer a low short-term price but compensate for it by future price increases. One such technique for durable goods manufacturers is to charge a low purchase price but have a high price for replacement parts—hence printers are cheap but ink cartridges are expensive. In the context of the 2008 financial crisis, teaser rates for mortgages, auto loans, and credit cards were indicted as one of the culprits of the crisis. The *Wall Street Journal* (2005) describes them as follows:

> Taking a page from credit-card companies and car makers, mortgage lenders are touting loans with rock-bottom introductory rates—in one case, nearly 0%. Most of these loans are so-called option adjustable-rate

mortgages, which carry an initial rate as low as 1%. One key and unusual feature: Borrowers get up to four payment choices each month. But the risks can be considerable and aren't always well understood. For one thing, the low introductory rate can last for as little as one to three months, after which the rate typically jumps above 4% or more. Plus, rates on these loans adjust frequently, meaning borrowers could see their costs rise as short-term interest rates increase. [...] Still, at IndyMac Bancorp, 30% of mortgage customers are opting for the company's Pay-Option ARM, which carries a starting rate of 1%.[9]

The policy response to such practices has been largely discretionary and indeed amounts to ex-post invalidation of private contracts. In December 2007 the Bush administration attempted to coerce lenders into freezing the adjustable rates for teaser mortgages.[10] More generally, we may imagine that in the future all sorts of regulations will prevent those practices.

▌ Markets as a Threat to the Paternalistic Organization of Society

Yet another conflict between markets and paternalistic governments is that the possibility of arbitrage brought about by markets may defeat the government's attempt to regulate the economy. This in turn may bring about further regulation, which may take the form of either more restrictions to the market or further preventive paternalistic measures.

Thus a forced savings scheme may be defeated by people simply borrowing against the future income generated by those savings. We may then expect policy to repress such attempts by making it illegal to borrow against one's future pension, implementing a tax on borrowing at certain ages, and so on.

People who ask managers of casinos to prevent their entry would always find some casino that would accept them if the gambling industry, instead of being tightly regulated, had free entry: there would always be some (perhaps online) casino that would not have signed a blocking contract with the individual on where he could go today. Similarly the Swedish paternalistic policy on alcohol sales relies on a state monopoly, the *Systembolaget*. Its outlets are few and far between, and have restrictive opening hours—contrast that with the density of wine sellers in Paris or London. Presumably, by imposing non-negligible physical upfront costs on people who want to buy liquor, the government hopes to deter compulsive purchases. The Swedish authorities are in conflict with the European Commission over this state monopoly which violates single-market rules. If the market for liquor sales were totally deregulated, the paternalistic policy could not be enforced. The government could then rely on a large sin tax.

---

[9] "Mortgage Teaser Rates Approach 0%," *Wall Street Journal*, February 15, 2005.
[10] "Bush freezes U.S. sub-prime mortgage rates," *The Times*, December 6, 2007.

Arguably this would be even more paternalistic, as it would harm responsible drinkers more than the Systembolaget would.[11]

If the government wishes to supply distorted information as a way to manipulate beliefs, it must also prevent a competitive market for information from operating. Otherwise reputable news sources would eventually emerge, and the government would be unable to control information.

▌ Market Interactions and Responsibility Transfer

Interactions through markets have effects on prices and thus consequences; this is another opportunity to extend the chain of preventive measures on consequentialist grounds. Remember that responsibility transfer applies to a chain of bilateral interactions between individuals whereby a licit action by one individual is penalized on the grounds of its negative consequences downward in the chain regardless of the agents' capacity for free will, consistency, and self-control. However, there is no reason to stop there and not extend the concept to anonymous impersonal interactions through supply and demand in markets for homogeneous products.

We already know that the paternalists think that if the product may be misused, this should be corrected by some sin tax that would artificially increase its price. In that case, why not consider the suppliers as liable for specific associated harms? This is indeed what many people believe. For example, there is a controversy in the United States as to whether baby bath seats should be prohibited on the grounds that parents are tempted not to look after their baby, which caused 120 deaths over a period of fifteen years. Similarly a 290-pound woman sued McDonald's because she had eaten too much at that restaurant.[12] Her attorney argued that McDonald's was faulty on two grounds. First, it did not provide a "healthy" alternative to its usual hamburger meals. Second, there should have been a (perhaps federally mandated) warning on those menus. In fact, such warnings are now compulsory in France. They take the form of Big-Brother–like slogans appended to any package or advertisement for certain types of food, such as "for your health, exercise regularly."

Even by their own standards, most paternalistic economists would dispute the first claim that the supplier of a particular product should be mandated to alter his product line in order to offer virtuous alternatives. This is likening the supplier to a state factory in a centrally planned economy. As long as the demand for the virtuous product exists, some firms will engage in that activity, and that does not have to be the producer of the vicious product, who presumably has neither the comparative advantage nor the required reputation for producing

---

[11] In our terminology, however, the Systembolaget is a strong form of paternalism, whereas taxes are weak paternalism. But this terminology refers to the nature of the instruments being used and not the intensity with which they are used.

[12] Again reported by Harsanyi 2007.

it. At best the paternalistic economist will want to subsidize the virtuous product, but even that is unclear since what matters for the consumer is the relative price between sin and virtue, so that this is redundant with the sin tax. The second claim has to do with the supplier's contractual obligation to give customers proper information on their product. It is known that the better that information is, the better identified products are and the more efficient the competitive market is. If the product characteristic is unobserved, then there is a so-called lemon problem[13] and markets may deliver the wrong outcomes and even disappear.[14] Thus mandated disclosure of the product characteristics may help restore efficiency, although it is often in the interests of firms to willingly release that information. Hence economists, whether or not they endorse behavioral approaches, are typically in favor of such regulations. However, although the producer is responsible for disclosing the nature of the product and the instructions for use, there is no reason why it should be liable for any conceivable misuse. But this occurs once the logic of responsibility transfer starts to operate.[15]

Making firms liable for unintended misuse of their products undermines the notion of common sense.[16] All societies rely on a common core of shared beliefs and expectations; for example, one does not put a living animal in a cooking device or people who weigh 290 pounds are abnormally fat and should do something about it. An implicit assumption in a market society is that in each transaction there is common knowledge between the parties that they are all endowed with common sense. Such an assumption is needed because, in its absence, the costs of specifying products, of writing contracts, and of resolving the litigations and errors involved in those processes are very large. Important resources would be wasted in the production of signals that have zero informational content for most of their recipients. The lower the core of accepted shared beliefs in a society, the more costly it is to operate markets and the less attractive

---

[13] Akerlof 1970.

[14] Essentially this is because a change in the price is also a signal for a change in quality, so that a single instrument—the price—has to perform two tasks: clearing the market by bringing supply and demand in line with each other, and conveying information about the product's quality.

[15] If individuals have behavioral biases, there is no simple solution to the problem of designing information about the product: What if many people are scared and overreact by not purchasing the product when it would be valuable to do so? What if they stop taking warnings seriously after having heard them too often and then ignore the most relevant ones? And, finally, one may be tempted to manipulate the information so as to offset the cognitive biases; but then this would trigger the wrong choices for rational individuals. Thus, despite the trend in the direction of an explosion of ludicrous warnings, it is no longer clear how information about the product characteristics should be regulated in a non-unitary world.

[16] Note that this is the result of responsibility transfer, which compels firms to explicitly consider unlikely events, and not to behavioral biases per se. A person can be perfectly rational and lack common sense (there is no dearth of such characters in academia); this simply means that such a person assumes less than others. Conversely, a person can have severe behavioral biases and a lot of common sense.

it will be to operate markets in a competitive, decentralized fashion, relative to a central planning solution.

The ultimate form of responsibility transfer is the notion of a "social right," which Mill criticized as a form of absolute tyranny. Participation in a market— say, by selling liquors—eventually shapes the social landscape through its consequences on the statistical prevalence of undesirable behaviors. Once the individuals who are responsible for those behaviors are no longer held accountable, the consequentialist view that the social landscape should be optimized by government interference in private transactions prevails. Thus Mill quotes the secretary of a prohibitionist alliance:

> If anything invades my social rights, certainly the traffic in strong drinks does. It destroys my primary right of security, by constantly creating and stimulating social disorder. [...] It impedes my right to free moral and intellectual development, by surrounding my path with dangers, and by weakening and demoralizing society, from which I have a right to claim mutual aid and intercourse.

A social right is a positive right for each individual to get the social environment he "deserves," and since there is a single social environment, short of splitting society into homogeneous clusters that do not interact with one another, this is inevitably conducive to conflict and tyranny.[17] Mill concludes: "The doctrine ascribes to all mankind a vested interest in each other's moral, intellectual and even physical perfection, to be defined by each claimant according to his own standard."

---

[17] An alternative, however, is to segregate society into homogeneous clubs that would each provide the most desired "social environment" to its members. This is in accordance with Tiebout's theory of clubs, and, arguably, society is moving in that direction, for example, through the increase in gated communities. Note that such an outcome can be reached by private contracting.

12

Where to Go?

Our discussion has revolved around the following argument: utilitarian foundations for limited government are quite shaky because they rest on the assumption of unitary, responsible individuals. Empirical deviations from that assumptions are numerous and well documented. This observation has led to a new brand of economics—happiness research and behavioral economics—which ends up typically advocating far more government involvement in private matters than the preceding brands of economics. At the same time we do observe an explosion of preventive laws that constrain a growing share of perfectly legitimate individual choices. While behavioral economics does not necessarily endorse all those policies, it does contribute to the trend by providing it with numerous foundations and justifications.

As a consequence, modern Western society faces a dilemma. One choice is to accept this evolution, and then not much imagination is needed to foresee a gradual elimination of individual freedom, as one progressively documents behavioral biases, measures happiness, and evaluates the effects of coercive policies, while information technology provides the government with ever more efficient tools of control. It is this process I have attempted to describe in this book. A second option is to reinstate strict boundaries to government intervention, and then the question is: On what basis?

Throughout the book I have consistently argued that denying the empirical relevance of behavioral biases is not an option. Some instrumental arguments, however, while accepting those findings, make the case that they cannot be used to justify an extension of government control over private lives. Let us discuss two of them.

The Internalization Argument

One general argument against paternalistic policies is that even though people have behavioral problems, they are mature enough to solve them on their own. This argument has two faces.

One version is that current incarnations can control the behavior of future ones, specifically by using appropriate contracts that commit those incarnations. Consider, for example, the undersaving problem associated with hyperbolic discounting. Individuals can achieve commitment on their own provided they can simply use illiquid assets that cannot be accessed by their future incarnations (unless these are remote enough in the future). Any money in a two-month deposit cannot be used by my incarnation next month; therefore my current incarnation can target quite precisely the consumption level of my next one by allocating its savings between liquid and illiquid assets. In fact, these instruments are too precise: relative to the absence of commitment, my incarnation next month is *harmed* if I can access illiquid assets!

In the numerical example at the end of chapter 6, Self 1 can replicate its dictatorial allocation by consuming 10, putting 5 in a two-period deposit, and leaving the rest in a one-period deposit. Self 2 will then be prevented from consuming more than 5. That will leave it with only 32.2 units of utility, which is clearly less than the no-commitment outcome. Government intervention cannot improve on that outcome. By restricting the use of illiquid assets, it could increase the welfare of my incarnation next month, but that would now come at the expense of my current incarnation. Clearly, in no way can my current incarnation be better off than if it is a dictator, and it can replicate that outcome provided it has access to two-period deposits.

If my current incarnation has access to enough financial instruments, and if the term structure of these instruments cannot be renegotiated away by my future selves, then the resulting allocation is Pareto optimal between selves. Therefore there is no scope for government intervention to make all selves better off, despite the fact that such intervention would generally lead to a different Pareto optimum than the one the government would pick up according to its social welfare function. In our numerical example, government intervention makes both Selves 1 and 2 better off relative to the no-commitment allocation; however, it makes Self 1 worse off and Self 2 better off relative to the replicated dictatorial allocation, which itself is worse than the no-commitment outcome for Self 2. Thus a paternalist who only cares about efficiency will be content with the use of financial instruments by the initial incarnation, whereas a true post-utilitarian who maximizes a weighted sum of the welfare level of different incarnations will typically disagree with the outcome.

Now one problem with this solution is that people may cheat on themselves. First of all, a court might let Incarnation 2 access the illiquid asset, either because it is treating the individual as unitary (in which case reneging on previous decisions must be the result of some new information having arrived and is efficient) or because it is treating the individual as non-unitary and concludes that the decisions of Incarnation 1 should not be binding on Incarnation 2. Second, Incarnation 2 can use the market to cheat by borrowing against the future earnings of the illiquid assets. This is another example of markets defeating paternalism through arbitrage. In this example, we see that markets can also defeat the paternalism that people impose on themselves. It is not clear how regulation could solve this. For example, if instead of a voluntary contract by Incarnation 1 we had a compulsory pension scheme, Self 2 might borrow against future pensions just the same. One could thus put restrictions on borrowing, but either they would not go far enough or they would severely hamper credit markets. For instance, precluding borrowing "against" future pensions just means that one could not seize those pensions in case of default. But the pension still makes the borrower solvent and, if the bank can find some other penalty that it may impose, the loan will go ahead.

Another version of the view that people can solve their behavioral problems themselves is the so-called Coasian view, that incarnations that coexist within the same individual may achieve an efficient outcome by bargaining between themselves.[1] They would thus sign an internal contract that would resolve the externalities exerted upon one another between the different incarnations, much in the same fashion as two neighbors reach an agreement about, say, when it is best for one of them to mow his lawn.

The Coasian argument is also unlikely to be palatable to the paternalists. To begin with, there is the usual problem that the internal distribution of welfare across incarnations, as an outcome of Coasian transactions, may be inconsistent with maximization of the post-utilitarian welfare function: the "Social Planner" may want to redistribute between incarnations of the same individual relative to the allocation obtained by Coasian bargaining.[2]

Next, there is the problem of enforceability: a contract between two different individuals is enforced by a third party (a court) on the basis of a suit by one of the parties who considers that the contract has been breached. It is difficult to see how this procedure could be extended to a contract between two incarnations of the same individual. The person would have to sign a contract with him- or herself, committing some future course of action, contingent on the circumstances. Then if those actions are not undertaken the very same individual would have to file a complaint against himself for not having implemented those actions. This sounds utterly absurd and so the contract would have to remain implicit, and, in any case, how would it be enforced?

But the fundamental objection that a paternalist would make is that Coasian bargaining is inconsistent with behavioral approaches. Much like it is not pos-

---

[1] See Whitman 2006.

[2] This actually opens up a difficult theoretical issue. We could make the case for a social welfare function such that "we" care about the relative standard of living of different individuals but not about the allocation of that standard of living between incarnations of the same individual, provided that allocation is efficient. Thus redistribution would reflect materialistic concerns for the physical consumption possibility set of people, whereas the government would remain totally indifferent to the relative happiness of competing incarnations within an individual. In such a world, there would be no disagreement between the social planner and the outcome of the internal Coasian bargaining, conditional on the total resources available to the individual.

sible to sign contracts now with future generations not yet born, I cannot bargain with my future selves if they do not exist today. Furthermore, the Coasian transaction itself is costly (it requires effort) and is therefore vulnerable to procrastination if there is hyperbolic discounting. Finally, because of other biases, such as cognitive dissonance and endowment effects, it is not obvious that the final transaction, if it exists, will be efficient. One incarnation, for example, may fail to compensate the other because of an endowment effect that it fails to see will be gone once the compensation has taken place.

The Agency Argument

Another class of arguments builds on the political economy critique. It states that while paternalism may help solve behavioral biases on paper, it ignores the actual working of governments. Thus the consequentialist approach should also be applied to the working of the government, and, as discussed by Glaeser (2005), it does not follow that recognition of behavioral issues justifies greater government intervention.

The argument is twofold. First, paternalistic policies endow the government with additional instruments that may then be used to pursue the agenda of private-interest groups at the expense of the general constituency—an issue already discussed in chapter 10. For example, as an infrastructure for manipulating beliefs for people's own good, is put in place, it may then be used by an incumbent government as a tool of propaganda to reduce votes for the opposition. Glaeser mentions, as an example, the promotion of the No Child Left Behind Act in the United States, which ended up "[promoting] the devotion of both the President and the Secretary of Education."

Second, the government is comprised of actual people who are themselves prone to behavioral biases. The case for paternalism then rests on whether bias is greater in government decisions versus private decisions. Glaeser proposes three mechanisms through which public decision making is more likely to suffer from errors than private decision making. First, whereas market participants are punished by competition and selection of the most rational strategies, bureaucrats do not face such discipline and therefore can indulge in compulsive behavior and cognitive dissonance to a greater extent. Second, private interests that wish to acquire influence by manipulating beliefs can do it at a lower cost, for a given leverage over actual decisions, under public decision making than under private decision making. Although under private decision making one must influence a large number of people in order to achieve a significant effect ("advertising"), only a few politicians and bureaucrats need to be convinced in order to impose a policy decision ("lobbying"). The latter will then be imposed on many people by law, so that lobbying will eventually have effects of the same order of magnitude as a massive advertising campaign, at a much lower cost. Third, elections only provide weak incentives for people to monitor the government (and acquire the relevant information), since everybody's vote is tiny and has a nearly zero chance of influencing the decision. By contrast, incentives to monitor oneself are far larger.

Even the assumption that governments obtain more objective information than people do is dubious. In theory, the government could use statistical analysis, experts, and studies to eschew the availability bias of private individuals and thus have a more objective view than voters. In practice, however, government decision makers have a limited time to devote to the experts and will also be subject to this bias, which opens the door for lobbying and other forms of manipulation.

These arguments suggest that behavioral economics, if anything, is a case for imposing greater constitutional limits on government.

To these points should be added the difficulty of even a well-intended, representative government to commit to its own policy course. The behavioral problems of the government were recognized well before those of the individuals. Governments have commitment problems in the same way that a "hyperbolic" individual does, as its horizon is limited by the next election and the constituency can always vote itself out of its previous commitments. For example, in the sin tax case, what prevents voters, presumably consisting of their current incarnation, from passing an immediate reduction in cigarette taxes in order to please their current selves?

Examples of inconsistent behavior from governments abound. The whole academic literature on rules versus discretion, initiated by Nobel Prize winners Kydland and Prescott, revolves around that issue. Governments are tempted to create inflation (i.e., to renege on a past commitment to price stability) in order to reduce the real value of public debt and to collect more revenues from the inflation tax. In the mid-twentieth century, private savings have been wiped out by such currency depreciation. In the 1960s and 1970s real interest rates were negative because of accelerating inflation. In the 2000s the French and German governments reneged on the Growth and Stability Pact (a very imperfect device aimed at lowering pressure on the European Central Bank to inflate by preventing individual countries from running excess deficits) the very day it would have become binding on them. Over a long period virtually no government has been able to invert the secular trend toward higher public expenditures. The necessity of pension reform means that previous commitments over the level and duration of pensions are, in fact, void, because these commitments were not feasible. So it is ironic that so many people envisage that the government could be of any help with regard to people's behavioral issues.

Beyond Instrumental Critiques

These instrumental arguments are not likely to be very convincing to the paternalists. They mostly open the door for endless empirical debates. For example, one can simply use documented outcomes, such as the same individual owning both low-interest savings accounts and high-interest credit card debt, as "proof" that the Coasian solution to behavioral biases is just not taking place. Or the above arguments that governments are more sensitive to errors can be opposed by the arguments of the previous chapter regarding how behavioral biases alter the efficiency of markets. Or the objection that voters have little economic incentives to acquire the relevant information in order to vote properly can be answered with the view that voters only need some intrinsic motivation to vote properly and that such motivation exists—otherwise most people would not vote at all.

In the end there is no presumption that the cost of government failure will be greater than the benefits of increased paternalism. And the costs can be reduced by writing rules governing the interventions of government officials; for example, France has a law restricting the use of computerized information. So again we have a case for limited government which is purely pragmatic instead of principled; it remains acceptable for Joseph K. to be prevented from using public transportation as long as we have enough checks and balances for such provisions to be used reasonably. That is obviously very different from thinking that Joseph K.'s right to use the train is nobody else's business.

Therefore, if we want to provide intellectual foundations for limited governments, we cannot do it merely on the basis of instrumental arguments. Instead, we need a system of values that delivers those limits and such a system cannot be utilitarian.

This book does not come close to delivering an answer, but let me offer some thoughts.

First, an "off-the-shelf" solution would be to opt for a strictly libertarian society where property rights and private contracts are sacred. If anything, Western societies are drifting away from such a model. In addition to the logical problem that such contracts and property rights must presumably be enforced by the state, which in turn must be financed by coercive taxation,[3] the issue emerges that such a society would let down those individuals who are too poor or unproductive to sustain themselves, which many citizens would find objectionable.

At the other extreme, however, we have shown that the current brand of paternalism increasingly intrudes on freedom and privacy for the sake of minor reductions in risks or minor statistical improvements in welfare (e.g., how many lives are saved by banning cigarette candies?). So a second solution we could

---

[3] The state is usually considered to have a comparative advantage in enforcing laws, property rights, and contracts, presumably because the law is a public good and these enforcement activities are a natural monopoly. See the discussion in Nozick 1975, pt. 1. Absent that, a world of competing laws and competing enforcers may resemble that described by Shleifer and Vishny (1993) in their paper on corruption where such competition is a form of rent seeking which drains resources out of productive activities and prevents economic development. Note, however, that some authors differ, most notably Friedman (1971).

envisage is a "hierarchy of social values" where survival would supersede freedom, but the latter would be of greater concern to society than statistical notions of public health or aggregate happiness.[4] This would allow for a minimal redistributive state that would rule out indigence, while most of the interventions falling under the label of strong paternalism would be out of the question because the kind of welfare that they allow people to achieve would be treated as secondary compared to individual freedom. For such an approach to be workable, some logical issues would have to be solved. For example, the grey zone of weak paternalism would have to be dealt with. Or one would have to explain why preventing misery is more justifiable than tolerating a rate of car accidents above the feasible minimum. In addition to these logical issues, one would have to bear with the lack of popularity of such conceptions. Currently most people in Western societies are not willing to accept that freedom and responsibility should be given more weight relative to happiness in the design of our institutions. Indeed, paternalistic governments are democratically elected and polls show substantial support for their policies. In 2004 the British Broadcasting Company reported a poll showing that, among Britons, "90% want healthier school meals; 66% want a smoking ban in public places; 80% want government action to ensure fruit and vegetables become cheaper; 72% want laws to limit salt, fat and sugar in foods; 73% want a stop on advertising junk foods to children; 72% want food labels informing them of nutritional value."[5]

Despite those objections, both the libertarian model and the hierarchy of social values model could replace the utilitarian one and form the basis of a political institution. In such a society, free will and individual responsibility are reaffirmed as central values that are not reducible to some aggregate objective. Limits to government do not stem from the fear that excess government intervention might get out of control and have harmful consequences but from

---

[4] Although Rawls's theory of justice is mostly consequentialist it does have a proviso for some values being "senior," which potentially could invalidate government interventions that would otherwise be justified on consequentialist (i.e., in Rawls's case, egalitarian) grounds.

Rawls's first principle of justice states that "each person is to have an equal right to the most extensive scheme of equal basic liberties compatible with a similar scheme of liberties for others." The second principle of justice is that "social and economic inequalities are to be arranged so that they are (a) reasonably expected to be to everyone's advantage," and (b) attach to positions and offices open to all." Then Rawls goes on to interpret his second principle as implying (i) Pareto-optimality, and (ii) that inequalities are justified only if they benefit the poorest group in society (the so-called difference principle). As I argued, this is a highly egalitarian interpretation of the second principle, which is not clearly implied by its original statement. Furthermore, while the second principle is trumped by the first, it is unclear how one would implement it practically without violating the first principle. For example, if one follows Nozick and believes that people are entitled to their property, and includes such entitlements in the "equal basic liberties," there is no way of implementing a redistributive policy without violating the first principle. Thus, while Rawls's two principles resemble a hierarchy of social values, the difference principle plays such a determinant role that the first principle becomes merely rhetorical.

[5] http://news.bbc.co.uk/1/hi/health/3839447.stm.

the principle that one cannot interfere with freedom of choice and individual responsibility.

An objection remains, however: Where does such a concern for freedom per se come from? After all, the utilitarian approach seems to derive social objectives endogenously from individual preferences, whereas here freedom as a value seems exogenously imposed. The first statement, of course, is excessive, since the way preferences are aggregated by a utilitarian social planner is itself exogenous. More fundamentally, however, it is impossible to provide a purely logical system of foundations for the organization of society independently of an opinion about human nature—this was already the case at the times of Locke and Hobbes, whose different views of mankind led them to advocate different political systems. For example, how can one reconcile the prevailing view that the government is in charge of social welfare with the view that it is not responsible for people's happiness but instead is just an agent in charge of some limited tasks well defined by a constitution, such as enforcing private contracts, law and order, and the provision of some well-defined public goods? In principle, both views may be conducive to workable societies. Let me conclude this book, however, by offering some subjective thoughts on why I believe that the post-utilitarian society rests on a flawed conception of human nature.

The behavioral biases are a second-order problem compared to how individuality is being constructed in an interactive fashion. As they grow up, people gradually define themselves in a way that is conditioned by their social environment; that is, they construct a persona which they choose from a menu of possibilities that is inevitably shaped by the social norms and role models to which they are confronted. Being treated by society as responsible and unitary goes a long way toward eliciting responsible and unitary behavior. The incentives to solve my own behavioral problems are much larger if I expect society to hold me responsible for the consequences of my actions. In other words, the personae that I can choose from the menu are typically consistent. Thus the merit of the liberal society is not that it allows people to optimally fulfill some preexisting needs but that, by imposing responsibility, it makes free will possible in a way compatible with the viability of society itself.

By contrast, the more society is paternalistic and based on non-unitary assumptions, the lower my incentives to construct a consistent persona and the more likely it is that I will abstain from signing Coasian contracts with myself, devising my own commitment devices, or acquiring relevant information and treating it rationally. The preventive measures may well bridle me at some point, but because I do not bear the consequences of my choices, I never have to think them through, and so there is no reason why I should establish a *plan* for my future course of actions. Examples abound that paternalistic preventive policies, coupled with the abolition of personal responsibility, are failing. One could mention the teenage pregnancy epidemic in the United Kingdom (despite much "counseling" going on in the educational system), the widespread use of drugs (despite their illegality), or the abdication of parental authority. In all those cases, the harmful consequences are taken care of by the government. Teenage mothers get welfare payments, drug addicts get treatment, and schools increasingly shed knowledge in favor of noncognitive and social skills.[6] If these developments are confirmed, the paternalistic society may eventually fail by its own standards and be abandoned. This would not be bad news to those who care about individual freedom.

[6] One may also think that learning from experience is a key component of the human experience. In the post-utilitarian society, such learning is supposed to be increasingly performed by scientific studies. People are no longer supposed to discover by themselves the good and the bad. Of course, from a utilitarian perspective, such a personal path to discovery has no merit.

References

Abel, A. 1990. "Asset Prices under Habit Formation and Catching Up with the Joneses." *American Economic Review* 80:38–42.

Akerlof, George A. 1970. "The Market for 'Lemons': Quality Uncertainty and the Market Mechanism." *Quarterly Journal of Economics* 84, no. 3: 488–500.

Akerlof, George A., and William T. Dickens. 1982. "The Economic Consequences of Cognitive Dissonance." *American Economic Review* 72, no. 3: 307–319.

Alesina, Alberto, Gerald Cohen, and Nouriel Roubini. 1997. *Political Cycles and the Macroeconomy.* Cambridge, Mass.: MIT Press.

Alesina, Alberto, Andrea Ichino, and Loukas Karabarbounis. 2007. "Gender-Based Taxation and the Division of Family Chores." National Bureau of Economic Research Working Paper No. 13638.

Arrow, Kenneth. 1963 [1951]. *Social Choice and Individual Values.* 2nd ed. New York: Wiley.

Atkeson, Andrew, and Robert E. Lucas. 1992. "On Efficient Distribution with Private Information." *Review of Economic Studies* 59: 427–453.

Barker, J. G., and R. J. Howell. 1992. "The Plethysmograph: A Review of Recent Literature." *Bulletin of the American Academy of Psychiatry and Law* 20, no. 1: 13–25.

Becker, Gary S., and Kevin M. Murphy. 1988. "A Theory of Rational Addiction." *Journal of Political Economy* 96, no. 4: 675–700.

Beevor, Anthony. 1998. *Stalingrad: The Fateful Siege, 1942–1943.* London: Viking.

Berridge, Kent C. 1996. "Food Reward: Brain Substrates of Wanting and Liking." *Neuroscience and Biobehavioral Reviews* 20, no. 1: 1–25.

Bertrand, Marianne, and Antoinette Schoar. 2003. "Managing with Style: The Effect of Managers on Firm Policies." *Quarterly Journal of Economics* 118, no. 4.

Bisin, Alberto, and Thierry Verdier. 2000. "Beyond the Melting Pot": Cultural Transmission, Marriage, and the Evolution of Ethnic and Religious Traits." *Quarterly Journal of Economics* 115, no. 3: 955–988.

Blanchard, Olivier, and Jean Tirole. 2008. "The Joint Design of Unemployment Insurance and Employment Protection: A First Pass." *Journal of the European Economic Association* 6, no. 1: 45–77.

Blanchflower, David G., and Andrew Oswald. 2000. "Well-being over Time in Britain and the U.S.A." Mimeograph, University of Warwick.

Brickman, Philip, Diana Coates, and Ronnie Janoff-Bulman. 1978. "Lottery Winners and Accident Victims: Is Happiness Relative?" *Journal of Personality and Social Psychology* 36, no. 8: 917–927.

Camerer, Colin, George Loewenstein, and Drazen Prelec. 2005. "Neuroeconomics: How Neuroscience Can Inform Economics." *Journal of Economic Literature* 43:9–64.

Choi, Stephen J., and A. C. Pritchard. 2003. "Behavioral Economics and the SEC." *Stanford Law Review* 56, no. 11: 1–74.

Chung, S. H., and Herrnstein, R. J. 1967. "Choice and Delay of Reinforcement." *Journal of the Experimental Analysis of Behavior* 10:67–64.

Compte, Olivier, and Andrew Postlewaite. 2004. "Confidence-Enhanced Performance." *American Economic Review* (December): 1536–1557.

Cunningham, Lawrence A. 2002. "Behavioral Finance and Investor Governance." *Washington and Lee Law Review* 59:767.

Davidson, R. J., D. C. Jackson, and N. H. Kalin. 2000. "Emotion, Plasticity, Context and Regulation: Perspectives from Affective Neuroscience." *Psychological Bulletin* 126: 890–906.

Dawkins, Richard. 1976. *The Selfish Gene.* New York: Oxford University Press.

de Meza, D., and J. R. Gould. 1992. "The Social Efficiency of Private Decisions to Enforce Property Rights." *Journal of Political Economy* 100:561–580.

Diamond, Peter. 2005. "Pensions for an Aging Population." Paper presented at the Institut d'Economie Industrielle (IDEI), Toulouse, Annual Conference. MIT Department of Economics Working Paper No. 05-33.

Drazen, Allan. 2001. *Political Economy in Macroeconomics.* Princeton, N.J.: Princeton University Press.

Duesenberry, James. 1952. *Income, Savings, and the Theory of Consumer Behaviour,* Cambridge, Mass.: Harvard University Press.

Easterlin, Richard A.. 2003. "Building a Better Theory of Well-being." Institut zur Zukunft der Arbeit (IZA) Working Paper No. 742.

Ellickson, Bryan, Birgit Grodal, Suzanne Scotchmer, and William R. Zame. 1999. "Clubs and the Market." *Econometrica* 67:1185–1218.

Farhi, Emmanuel, and Ivan Werning. 2005. "Inequality, Social Discounting, and Estate Taxation." National Bureau of Economic Research Working Paper No. 11408.

Feldstein, Martin. 1976. "Temporary Layoffs in the Theory of Unemployment." *Journal of Political Economy* 84:937–957.

Frank, Robert H. 1997. "The Frame of Reference as a Public Good." *Economic Journal* 107, no. 445: 1832–1847.

Frey, Bruno S., and Mathias Benz. 2001. "Motivation Transfer Effect." mimeo, University of Zürich.

Friedman, David. 1971. *The Machinery of Freedom.* New York: Harper and Row.

Glaeser, Edward. 2005. "Paternalism and Psychology," Harvard Institute of Economic Research Discussion Paper No. 2097.

Grochulski, Borys, and Narayana Kocherlakota. 2007. "Nonseparable Preferences and Optimal Social Security Systems." National Bureau of Economic Research Working Paper No. 13362.

Harsanyi, David. 2007. *Nanny State.* New York: Broadway Books.

Hanushek, E. 2002. "Publicly Provided Education." In A. J. Auerbach and M. Feldstein, eds., *Handbook of Public Economics,* chap. 30. Amsterdam: North-Holland.

Haskell, Jonathan, and Holger Wolf. "The Law of One Price: A Case Study." *Scandinavian Journal of Economics* 103, no. 4: 545–558.

Hayek, Friedrich. 1937. "Economics and Knowledge." *Economica* 4, no. 13: 33–54.

———. 1940. "The Competitive "Solution"," *Economica*, 7, 26, 125–149.

———. 1944. *The Road to Serfdom*. London: Routledge.

Heath, C., and J. B. Soll 1996. "Mental Budgeting and Consumer Decisions," *Journal of Consumer Research* 23, no. 1: 40–52

Helliwell, J. 2001. "How Is Life? Combining Individual and National Variables to Explain Subjective Well-being." National Bureau of Economic Research Working Paper No. 9065.

Inglehart, R., and H-D. Klingemann. 2000. "Genes, Culture, Democracy and Happiness." In E. Diener and E. M. Suh, eds., *Culture and Subjective Well-being*. Cambridge, Mass.: MIT Press.

Kahneman, Daniel, and Amos Tversky. 1972. "Subjective Probability: A Judgment of Representativeness." *Cognitive Psychology* 3:430–454.

———. 1979 "Prospect Theory: An Analysis of Decision under Risk." *Econometrica* 47:263–291.

Kahneman, Daniel, Jack Knetsch, and Richard Thaler. 1990. "Experimental Tests of the Endowment Effect and the Coase Theorem." *Journal of Political Economy* 98, no. 6: 1325–1348.

Kendall, Todd. 2007. "Pornography, Rape, and the Internet." Paper presented at the Toulouse Conference on the Economics of Software and the Internet, January.

Laibson, David. 1997. "Golden Eggs and Hyperbolic Discounting." *Quarterly Journal of Economics* 112, no. 2: 443–477.

Lamont, Owen, and Richard Thaler. 2003. "Anomalies: The Law of One Price in Financial Markets." *Journal of Economic Perspectives* 17, no. 4: 191–202.

Lange, Oskar. 1936. "On the Economic Theory of Socialism." *Review of Economic Studies* 4, no. 1: 53–71.

Laroque, Guy, and Bernard Salanié. 2002. "Labour Market Institutions and Employment in France." *Journal of Applied Econometrics* 17, no. 1: 25–48.

Layard, Richard. 2003. *Happiness: Has Social Science a Clue?* Lionel Robbins Lectures, London School of Economics.

———. 2007. "Happiness and the Teaching of Values." *CentrePiece* (summer): 18–23.

Lee, Han, and Ulrike Malmendier. 2007. "The Bidder's Curse." National Bureau of Economic Research Working Paper No. W13699.

Lord, Charles G., Lee Ross, and Mark R. Lepper. 1979. "Biased Assimilation and Attitude Polarization: The Effects of Prior Theories on Subsequently Considered Evidence," *Journal of Personality and Social Psychology* 37, no. 11: 2098–2109.

Malmendier, Ulrike, and Geoffrey Tate. 2005. "CEO Overconfidence and Corporate Investment." *Journal of Finance* 60, no. 6: 2661–2700.

Mill, John Suart. 1863. *On Liberty*. 2nd ed. Boston: Ticknor and Fields.

Mirrlees, James. 1971. "An Exploration in the Theory of Optimum Income Taxation." *Review of Economic Studies* 38, no. 114: 175–208.

Mises, Ludwig von. 1920. "Die Wirtschaftsrechnung im sozialistischen Gemeinwesen." *Archiv für Sozialwissenschaften* 47. Translated in F. A. Hayek, ed., *Collectivist Economic Planning* (London: Routledge, 1935; reprint, Clifton, N.J.: Augustus M. Kelley, 1975).

Neumann, Johannes von, and Oskar Morgenstern. 1954. *Theory of Games and Economic Behavior*. Princeton, N.J.: Princeton University Press.

Nozick, Robert. 1974, *Anarchy, State, and Utopia,* New York: Basic Books.

Odean, Terrance. 1998. "Volume, Volatility, Price, and Profit When All Traders Are above Average." *Journal of Finance* 53, no. 6: 1887–1934.

O'Donoghue, Ted, and Matthew Rabin. 2003. "Studying Optimal Paternalism, Illustrated by a Model of Sin Taxes." *American Economic Review* 93, no. 2: 186–191

Persson, Torsten, and Guido Tabellini. 2000. *Political Economics: Explaining Economic Policy.* Cambridge, Mass.: MIT Press.

Phelps, Edmund S. 1994. *Structural Slumps,* Cambridge MA: Harvard University Press.

Pigou, A. C. 1920. *The Economics of Welfare.* London: McMillan.

Rainwater, Lee. 1994. "Family Equivalence as a Social Construction." In D. Ekert-Jaffe, ed., *Standards of Living and Families: Observation and Analysis,* 25–39. Montrouge: John Libbey Eurotext.

Rasmussen, Douglas, and Douglas J. Den Uyl. 2005. *Norms of Liberty: A Perfectionist Basis for Non-Perfectionist Politics.* University Park: Pennsylvania State University Press.

Rawls, John. 1971. *A Theory of Justice,* Cambridge, Mass.: Harvard University Press.

Ross, H. Laurence. 1984. "Social Control through Deterrence: Drinking-and-Driving Laws." *Annual Review of Sociology* 10:21–35.

Ross, Lee, Mark R. Leppner, and Michael Hubbard. 1995. "Perseverance in Self-Perception and Social Perception : Biased Attributional Processes in the Debriefing Paradigm." *Journal of Personality and Social Psychology* 32, no. 5: 880–892.

Saint-Paul, Gilles. 2002. "Cognitive Ability and Paternalism." Centre for Economic Policy Research Working Paper No 3642.

———. 2007. "How Does the Allocation of Credit Select between Boundedly Rational Firms?" *Journal of the European Economic Association* 5, no. 2–3): 411–419.

———. 2008. "Against Gender-Based Taxation," Centre for Economic Policy Research Working Paper No. 6582.

Salanié, François, and Nicolas Treich. 2009. "Regulation in Happyville." *Economic Journal* 119, no. 537: 665–679

Savage, L. 1954. *The Foundations of Statistics.* New York: Wiley.

Sheshinski, Eytan. 2002. "Bounded Rationality and Socially Optimal Limits on Choice in a Self-Selection Model." Hebrew University Working Paper No. 330.

Shleifer, Andrei, and Vishny, Robert W. 1993. "Corruption." *Quarterly Journal of Economics* 108, no. 3: 599–617.

Simon, Walter T., and Peter G. Schouten. 1991. "Plethysmography in the Assessment and Treatment of Sexual Deviancy: An Overview." *Archives of Sexual Behavior* 20, no. 1: 76–85.

Solnick, S. J., and D. Hemenway. 1998. "Is More Always Better? A Survey on Positional Concerns." *Journal of Economic Behaviour and Organisation* 37:373–383.

Stiglitz, Joseph E. 1984. "Price Rigidities and Market Structure." *American Economic Review* 64:350–355.

Sunstein, Cass R. 1997. "Behavioral Analysis of Law." *University of Chicago Law Review* 64, no. 4: 1175–1195.

Thaler, Richard H. "Toward a Positive Theory of Consumer Choice." *Journal of Economic Behavior and Organization* 1, no. 1: 39–60.

Thaler, Richard H., and Cass R. Sunstein. "Libertarian Paternalism." *American Economic Review* 93, no. 2: 175–179.

Tiebout, C. 1956. "A Pure Theory of Local Expenditures." *Journal of Political Economy* 64 no. 5: 416–424.

Tversky, A., and D. Kahneman. 1971. "The Belief in the Law of Small Numbers." *Psychological Bulletin* 76:105–110.

Volokh, Eugene. 1997. "What Speech Does "Hostile Work Environment" Harassment Law Restrict?" 85 *Georgetown Law Journal* 627.

Weitzman, Martin. 1974. "Prices vs. Quantities." *Review of Economic Studies* 41, no. 4: 477–491.

Weyl, Glen. 2009. "Whose Rights? A Critique of Individual Agency as the Basis of Rights." *Politics, Philosophy and Economics* 8, no. 2: 139–171.

Whitman, Glen. 2006. "Against the New Paternalism: Internalities and the Economics of Self-Control." Policy Analysis No. 563, Cato Institute, February 22, 1–16.

Index

Abel, 49
addiction, 24, 49, 78–80, 131, 141; rational, 24, 49, 65
Aeschylus, 10
Akerlof, 78, 144n13
akrasia, 15, 18
Alesina, A., 39n30, 111n15
Allen, Woody, 16n3
altruism, 28
anti-social behavior order, *see* ASBO
arguments, instrumental, 38–39, 99, 102, 124, 126, 146; principled, 39
Aristotle, 7, 15
Arrow, K., 39n31
ASBO, 103–104, 109–110
Ashley, J., 111
Atkeson, 33n17
availability bias, 42, 85, 138, 150

Barker, 126n2
Becker, G. 24
Benda, J., 79
Benz, 47
Berridge, 17
Bertrand, M., 137n4
Bisin, 87
Blanchard, 33n19
Blanchflower, 53, 54n2
Blomberg, J., 121
brain, activity, 17–18, 52; processes, 16–18, 20, 50
Brickman, 49
Buffet, W., 139
Bush, G. W., 142

Camerer, C., 16n2, 17
Choi, 137, 139
Chung, 44n3

Coasian critique, argument, 70n7, 72n9, 148–149, 151, 153
Coates, 49
cognitive dissonance, 42–43, 78, 86, 91, 95, 135, 138, 149
Compte, 50
Comte, A.,128
concave, concavity: *see* utility function
Condorcet paradox, 39n31; jury theorem, 129
confidence-enhanced performance, 49–50, 86
consequentialism, 38, 40n32, 73, 77, 87, 100–101, 115–117, 125, 125n1, 143, 145, 149, 152n4
context effects, 47–49, 84
Cunningham, 108, 138, 139n7

Dal, G., 99
Davidson, 52
Dawkins, 58n7
default options, 48
Den Uyl, 39n29
Diamond, 84n5
Dickens, 78
discounting: discount rate, 44, 98; hyperbolic discounting, 44–46, 57n6, 66n2, 68–69, 98, 135, 141, 147, 149–150
Drazen, A., 39n30
Dubois, P., 99
Duesenberry, J., 48
dynamic social contract theory, 33–34, 92–93

Easterlin, 51–53, 82n5
Ellickson, 31n11
endowment effect, 48, 82, 85, 141, 149
excludability, 72
externality, 30–32, 66–67, 72–73, 77, 81–83, 87–89, 92–94, 130